D1320335

Spiritual Secrets
of Famous Christians

SPIRITUAL SECRETS

OF

FAMOUS CHRISTIANS

by
ANNA TALBOTT McPHERSON
Author of *Forgotten Saints*

ZONDERVAN PUBLISHING HOUSE
GRAND RAPIDS, MICHIGAN

Foreword

As in writing *Forgotten Saints,* so now in sketching the characters of these better known men and women of God, my hope is that their exalted other-world living may be unveiled in such a manner that it will be an inspiration to all those, young and old, who pant for a deep breath of the pure, free air of heights celestial, and who, through fiery self-crucifixion, such as obsessed the saints introduced herein, seek a crown incorruptible, an inheritance among them who are sanctified.

I have written, not primarily to pay tribute to the characters themselves, but to reveal the exceeding grace of God in them, that grace which is just as free to you and me as it was to them, *if* we are but willing to go to the same length of sacrifice.

May we of this generation, beholding the glorious example of these choice ones whose meat and drink was God Himself, be challenged to relinquish all earthiness and that which wars against the spirit; be challenged to become a separate people, dedicated heart and soul to the pursuit of holiness unto the Lord.

ANNA TALBOTT McPHERSON

Damascus, Ohio

Contents

Foreword

Heroine to the End

THE HASSELTINE HOMESTEAD stood pleasantly beside "Boston Road" near Bradford, Massachusetts. It was one of those New England homes whose cheery hospitality had become so much a part of the social life of the countryside around that people took it for granted.

This twenty-ninth day of June, 1810, its doors and windows were wide open to the golden sunshine, and to the caroling of songbirds on the shady lawn. The usual sense of welcome was intensified by an extraordinary bustling about in the kitchen.

"There," Mother breathed with satisfaction. Her round face was flushed with the heat of the great brick oven by the fireplace. "The fowl is browned to a turn, so are the biscuits. Rebecca, are the vegetables done? Mary, 'tis time to draw fresh cold water from the spring. Abbie, thee stay with me to dish up the victuals as soon as . . . Nancy, does thee see them coming?"

Mother kept her eye on the potatoes snapping in the ashes, the teakettle swinging on the crane.

Nancy, whose real name was Ann, was standing in the doorway. Now she peered down the winding road, one hand shading her large brown eyes. "I believe so, Mother," she answered politely. "Yes, they must be. There is a group of people, and Father in the midst."

"The ministers, or mayhap the missionary volunteers," Mother decided. "Here, Abbie, quickly! the platter and the carving knife."

Each one hurried to her task. Nancy made one last round of inspection in the large west dining room. Yes, everything was ready there. The snowy white cloth, the exquisitely designed sugar and creamer which had been brought from England by her grandmother, the heirloom silver, the napkins in their holders, the stack of china at Father's place, all ready to be served.

The sound of men's eager, enthusiastic voices drew nearer. Now the group entered the gateway. Father was speaking.

9

"A daring undertaking, but a worthy one indeed!" Nancy heard him say.

"We would better not try to stop God," one of the ministers ventured.

"No," said still another. "If these are willing to go, 'tis but a small task laid on our shoulders — that of sending them."

Nancy must meet the men at the door, take their hats and show them to their places. Her cheeks blushed as prettily as the roses climbing over the doorway, and tiny soft curls clustered about her fair neck. She knew what the talk was about. The annual Massachusetts ministers' session had been electrified the day before by the proposition of four young Andover Theological Seminary students that the New England parish send them as missionaries to the heathen in Asia. Never before had a missionary gone from America to countries beyond the seas, months and months away. Upon first thought most of the ministers considered the undertaking as "wild and romantic," yet the young men persisted in the conviction that God had spoken, and now it sounded to Nancy as though they might be gaining their point.

In came the men. Nancy greeted each one with gracious words and proper manners. So excited was she that she scarcely saw individuals at all. They were just a blur of strangers whom she must make welcome.

"Be seated, Brethren," Father was saying.

Mother was already bringing the steaming platter of meat. Nancy turned from the doorway to serve her father's guests, when suddenly she became aware of a tall form beside her. She looked up. A pair of keen, fearless brown eyes met hers. For one sweet moment they lingered looking at one another — a young man and a maiden, held spellbound. Then with a shy smile, the girl turned to her duties at the table.

Nancy had heard Father tell of Adoniram Judson, the spokesman of the missionary volunteers. This must be he. Strange though, how preoccupied he was with his plate during the meal. The report had been that he was a brilliant conversationalist and ready of wit. Now he was unaccountably silent.

Nancy cut the pies set out in a row on the broad windowsill, and stole a glance now and then at the young man who was supposed to be the hero of the hour. Little did she dream that at that very moment he was composing a graceful sonnet in her praise!

The group of ministers and young Mr. Judson went back

to their deliberation at the church leaving Nancy with nothing more definite to think about than the bewitching searchings of a young man's brown eyes and his puzzling behavior thereafter.

Nearly a month passed by before the Boston stage-coach brought to "Miss Ann Hasseltine, Bradford, Massachusetts," a letter addressed in the large, honest handwriting of the daring young missionary volunteer. Nancy blushed as her sisters all crowded about her to know what this might mean. But the missive was held jealously to her bosom, and not until she had locked herself in her own bedchamber did she dare to break the seal. The girl's eyes were at first eager, then wondering, and finally with tears they dreamily looked out of her window toward the Merrimac River, then eastward to the ocean and still farther out to more distant horizons still.

Nancy slid to her knees with the astounding letter laid out before her on the great oak chest by the window. The proposition had been short and to the point. Adoniram Judson had asked her to marry him and go as a missioinary to far-away India!

Hardly did she recognize her own thoughts nor the meaning of the extraordinary thumping within her breast. Was she the same Ann Hasseltine that until her seventeenth year had been the life of all the social gatherings of the village, the one most frivolous and carefree? If Adoniram had known how her former years had been so entirely consumed with interest in party dresses and party happenings, how all through her early youth she had considered herself too old to say her prayers! — would he ask her now to become a missionary?

She was still Ann Hasseltine, to be sure, but she was a new Ann. Four years ago she had found the Saviour and everything had become changed. Since that momentous happening she had wanted nothing so much as to venture all for Jesus, cost what it may. Now this letter gave her the chance to prove her loyalty. She did not wince. Something in the thought of risking all to serve her Master on the other side of the world took possession of Nancy altogether. Still, she did not answer Adoniram at once. And what thoughtful girl would?

No woman had ever yet crossed the sea to become a missionary in Asia. The ocean voyage was long and perilous; the climate of India was unfavorable; the language and customs loomed up as forbidding obstacles at the very outset; danger of violence at the hands of the natives was ominous; and there was no prospect of ever coming home!

But after only two months of soul-searching and prayer, Ann Hasseltine's father gave consent, and the girl's own heart and pen said, "Yes," to the proffer of the hand of the young missionary volunteer and to an equal share in his fortune.

Ann and Adoniram set sail upon the bleak Atlantic on February 19, 1812. When they landed in Calcutta the following June, the East India Company promptly turned its hostile eye upon them and forced them out of the country. For a whole year they wandered o'er land and sea in weary, anxious search for some spot they would be allowed to call home.

It was June 20, 1813, that Ann wrote in her diary, "We have at last concluded, in our distress, to go to Rangoon (Burma), as there is no vessel about to sail for any other place ere it will be too late to escape . . . arrest."

It had been a heroic decision, for Burma was indeed a wild, barbaric country, outside a civilized government, inside a despotic monarchy of the most merciless variety.

Ann continued, "I have been accustomed to view this field of labor with dread and terror, but I now feel perfectly willing to make it my home the rest of my life . . . Adieus to polished, refined, Christian society. Our lot is not cast among you, but among pagans, among barbarians, whose tender mercies are cruel. Indeed, we voluntarily forsake you and for Jesus' sake choose the latter for our associates."

The young missionaries' most dismal apprehension, however, had not equaled the sight that confronted them as they entered Rangoon in July. Its waterfront presented the aspect of a vast, sludgy swamp covered with tumble-down bamboo huts built on poles above the muck and mire. As far as eye could see there was dilapidation, neglect and filth.

Terror stabbed the hearts of Ann and Adoniram, but as they prayed, God sent peace on the wings of His Word, "Although I have cast them far off among the heathen, and although I have scattered them among the countries, yet will I be to them as a little sanctuary in the countries where they shall come."

Many times was Ann to find herself leaning heavily upon this promise for comfort in her loneliness. For it was to be two and a half years before she would receive her first letter from loved ones in America, and ten years before her first visit home. During these ten years many strange and difficult experiences were hers as she labored to master an extremely intricate language, and to accustom herself to the ways of a heathen people.

During this time, too, Baby Roger Williams Judson was born, and after only a few months died, leaving her heart torn and broken.

But there were other things to remember about those ten years which filled Ann's heart with gladness. A wayside chapel of bamboo and thatch had been built by Adoniram on one of the pagoda roads in Rangoon, where now a stalwart little band of disciples, members of the church, twelve in all, worshiped every Sabbath day. Here too, Ann herself had been conducting a Wednesday evening Bible Class, and the memories of those sacred hours were cherished indeed.

When in June, 1823, after her first visit home, Ann again embarked for the Orient, a strange foreboding told her she was leaving never to return. Nevertheless, she departed with a light heart and an indescribable yearning to enter again into her ministry among the beloved converts in Rangoon. Five more had been added to the little band in her absence, and her faith took hold for great things ahead.

But Ann's stay in Rangoon was to be short-lived. New missionaries had arrived, sufficient in number to care for the growing mission there. Adoniram, encouraged by the king's invitation to found a Christian mission in Ava, the capital city of the Burmese Empire, felt that he must press on to claim another heathen city for the one true God.

Before they reached the "golden city" in February, 1824, however, they were confronted with grim bafflement. Hearing of their approach, Dr. Price, who had gone on before, came in a small boat to meet them and to warn them that the tide of popularity had seemed to turn suddenly against foreigners in Ava, because of imminent war with Great Britain.

On the twenty-third of May, the message came to the little group at Ava that Rangoon had been captured by the British army. War had actually begun! And foreigners in Ava were face to face with its awful uncertainties.

The missionaries were not long in feeling the effects of the hostilities. One June day as Ann and Adoniram were about to seat themselves at the dinner table, the door suddenly burst open and an officer demanded, "Where's the teacher?"

Adoniram stepped forward.

"You are wanted by the king!" shouted the jailor and executioner, for so he proved to be.

Instantly Adoniram was thrown to the floor, bound and

dragged away, in spite of Ann's repeated offers of money for his release. From the courthouse he was forced to the death prison, and up high steps to one, dark, filthy room, the chamber of horrors. Here he was to be forbidden but rarely to speak to his fellow prisoners or to communicate with friends outside. Many times he would be compelled to pay bribes for the delivery of his food, and would be denied water and fresh clothing. Three pairs of fetters galled his ankles, and so closely was he bound that he could shuffle around only a few inches at a time. Constantly he was tortured by the sound of the piteous cries of some fellow prisoner being whipped with cords or beaten by an iron mallet, or worse still, led forth at the fatal hour of three in the afternoon for execution.

From this time on, Ann's life became a series of maneuvers for the rescue of her husband and other foreign prisoners which caused her to be known far and wide as the "heroine of Ava."

Scarcely a day passed without a visit to some member of the royal family or government staff to plead for the prisoners. Daily, when not roughly prohibited, she visited her husband, giving him what food and clothing she could procure, since for the most part he was entirely dependent upon her for these necessities.

"She stood at the prison gate like a queen," Adoniram told a colleague later. "Many times she was allowed to visit me only at night. They told me how she walked through the streets of Ava at the darkest hours protected by an almost enchanted dignity, and how her matchless courage won the hearts of jailors and nobles alike."

For seven months this unthinkable state of affairs persisted until one day Ann was missing from the audience room of the governor and from the prison gate. For almost three weeks she was absent, then when she did return, she carried in her arms the wee form of her newborn child, Baby Maria. So overjoyed was Adoniram to see his wife and babe, that amid much pain and difficulty he crawled forth to take his child for the first time in his arms. Afterwards, during his lonely hours in prison he composed twenty-four stanzas of poetry in her honor.

This joy, however, was only a slight calm in the mighty sea of misfortune upon which the Judsons were embarked. When Maria was little more than three months old, a servant came running to Ann one morning, his face pale with fright.

"The white prisoners have all been carried away," he gasped.

"Away?" choked Ann. "Away where?"

The messenger could give her no answer.

Distractedly she ran into the street looking first this way, then that. But no sight of her husband and his comrades was to be seen. She dashed down one street, then another.

"Which way did the prisoners go?" she asked everyone she met. Finally an old woman ventured a clue.

"They're on their way to Amarapoora down the river," she whispered.

Ann lost no time in gathering relief supplies and other things necessary for the journey. With her baby in her arms she set out for Amarapoora, first in a boat, then by oxcart. Arriving travelworn and anxious, she found that the prisoners had been sent four miles further on, to the village of Aungbinle.

With her baby in her arms, she set out

Ann followed. And late in the afternoon she found Adoniram in the village prison, weak and pale, after the cruel sufferings of his tortuous march.

Not being permitted to put up her own little bamboo house near the prison, Ann took refuge in a little room half filled with grain and accumulated dirt. Here she was to stay for many successive days and nights, for, having spent her strength to the limit of physical endurance, she was prostrated by a miserable tropical disease, and lay helpless on her thin, shabby mat on the floor for two months.

Night after night the sick mother's heart was torn by the pitiful wails of her baby crying for the food which she could not supply. Finally by sending gifts to the jailors, she won for her husband the permission to carry the baby through the village and beg a few drops of nourishment to sustain it, first from one Burmese mother, then another.

After six months of this unspeakable way of life in Aungbinle, Adoniram was suddenly released. But hopes of normal existence again were short-lived, for the young missionary was sent forthwith to Maloun as an interpreter for the Burman army, and Ann, completely exhausted, fell a prey to that dreaded malady, spotted fever.

During her utter helplessness and delirium, God manifested his watchful care in a miraculous way. First, without solicitation, a Burmese woman offered to care for and to nurse Baby Maria. Then, just when the last of Ann's strength was ebbing away and the Burmese neighbors had gathered to see her die, Dr. Price was released from prison and hastened to her bedside.

After the most desperate measures were taken to revive her, Ann slowly took a new hold on life, only to find that her husband had been imprisoned again.

She could scarcely breathe.

"I could not rise from my couch," she wrote to a friend later, "I could make no efforts to secure my husband; I could only plead with that great and powerful Being who has said, 'Call upon me in the day of trouble, and I will hear, and thou shalt glorify me,' and who made me at this time feel so powerfully this promise, that I became quite composed, feeling assured that my prayers would be answered."

She sent a servant to make one more appeal to the governor. The governor sent a petition to the high court of the empire, and lo, Adoniram was released.

He rushed to his home, with thoughts of Ann at the door waiting for him, the babe in her arms.

The door of his house indeed stood open, but Ann was not there to greet him. He entered. There was no one in the first room except a half-clothed Burmese woman, crouching before a little fire, holding in her arms a puny little baby grimy with dirt. Not for a moment did Adoniram dream that this emaciated baby could be his, so he hurried on to the next room. Lying across the foot of the bed as though she had fallen there, was Ann. Her face was pale and drawn, her whole form shrunken and broken. Her curls had been cut off during her illness and now an old cotton cap covered her head.

"Ann," her husband breathed softly, "Ann."

The form stirred slightly, the brown eyes opened. And Ann looked unbelievingly, wonderingly, into the eyes of her beloved husband.

❀   ❀   ❀   ❀   ❀

In a matter of weeks, war was ended, and the Judsons were freed from the cruelties of Ava. The only course left seemed to be to return to Rangoon and continue work among their little group in that place. The Burmese Christians had scattered in alarm when war befell their city, but four now gathered to welcome the Judsons back and to pledge their loyalty in helping to build anew the shattered little mission.

It was no longer necessary to live under the Burmese government in order to live among the Burmese people, for, in the war, Great Britain had secured a long strip of the Burmese seacoast. In this territory then, at Amherst, the Judsons and their four Burmese Christians created a wilderness home and mission in the summer of 1826.

Even here, however, Ann and Adoniram were not to be at rest. In the anticipation that his presence would be of help in insuring religious liberty to the subjects of Burma, Adoniram was prevailed upon to accompany the British Civil Commissioner to Ava in the capacity of British ambassador.

Again Ann and Adoniram said good-by, this time in the hope of being reunited in a few weeks to continue their beloved work in Amherst, unmolested.

They hoped in vain.

While Adoniram was absent on this mission, Ann fell victim to another fever which proved to be too vicious. On the sixth of October, 1826, her spirit went home to God, torn from her husband's bleeding heart and from her babe.

Before she went, she said plaintively, "The teacher (Adoniram) is long in coming; and the new missionaries are long in coming; I must die alone and leave my little one." Then she brightened, and a light stole softly upon her face. It was a light that told of courage — of a faith in One above who doeth all things well. "But as it is the will of God," she continued radiantly, "I acquiesce in his will."

It was this that made Ann the heroine she was. Not primarily that she had suffered triumphantly the afflictions that had dogged her pathway throughout her stay in Burma, but that she had accepted them as being a part of God's plan and that she had no complaints to make. His will was her will and in it she was supremely happy.

One of the greatest joys Ann experienced in her last few days on earth was to learn that her husband's unfinished manuscript of the Burman Bible, upon which he had spent ten years of toilsome labor, and which she had concealed within the old pillow used by her husband in prison, had been miraculously found and kept for them through all the ravages of war, by an old servant. She did not live to see the time, however, when Adoniram, eight years later, finished translating the entire Bible into Burmese. This Bible is to the Burmese what Luther's is to the Germans, and the King James version to the English. Neither did she see, out of their small attempts in Christian education, the Rangoon Baptist College come into existence, with its one thousand students pouring in from all corners of the empire. Working with a simple hand press to issue their primitive publications, she did not live to see the well-equipped printing establishment, known as the American Baptist Mission Press, become a reality in Burma. And springing from their little church of three or four members after the war, she did not see the one hundred fifty-eight organized churches with a membership of nearly ten thousand, which are now within the boundaries of Rangoon.

No, Ann was not permitted to see all the fruits of her labors and unspeakable sufferings in Burma, but she walked by faith, and in this was well content. In this lay her heroism.

"Blessed are they," said the Master, "who have not seen, and yet have believed."

The Unpredictable Peter Cartwright

SILHOUETTED AGAINST THE flaming Tennessee sunset of a June evening in 1820 rode a lone figure on horseback. The square, two hundred pound frame of the rider betokened considerable physical vigor, of which the owner said, in substance, "God gave me a good constitution — one that will wear out a dozen threshing machines. He knew I would need it when He chose me to be one of His breaking plows."

It was Saturday night, and the lone equestrian, Peter Cartwright, was en route to his home in Christian County in southwest Kentucky, having parted with a traveling companion at Knoxville, Tennessee, as they journeyed westward from the Methodist General Conference in Baltimore. He found himself in a rugged region of country. Hills, knobs and spurs of the Cumberland mountains cast their shadows in the valleys and obliterated all trace of the path he must travel, except for the few feet in advance of his horse's nodding head which were still visible in the fast-fading sunlight.

"How I would like to find the cabin of some Christian people," he said, half to his horse and half to himself, "and spend the Sabbath with them. But it is hardly possible." He sighed. And then, as if to explain to his steed, he went on, "There is no gospel preacher for miles around, and many of these poor people have never heard a gospel message in all their lives. All they know of the Sabbath is to hunt and visit, drink and dance."

Thus, lonesome and pensive, Peter Cartwright, late in the dusk, drew up to a sign bearing the crudely painted information that the house up the lane "kept entertainment." He approached the "tolerably decent" building and asked for lodging.

"Sure, you can stay," the proprietor began. Then he hesitated. "I'm afraid, though, you're not going to enjoy yourself much. That is, if you want to go to sleep right soon. You see, there's a party meeting here tonight to have a little dance."

19

Disappointment plainly clouded the traveler's face. "How far is it to the next decent place?" he queried.

"Seven miles."

"Seven miles . . . A long way in the dark over a strange path. If you'll treat me civilly and feed my horse well, I believe I'll just stay here."

"You'll be welcome, friend," assured the mountaineer, "We'll do our best by you, sure."

Peter Cartwright dismounted, entered the cabin, and after a simple meal, quietly took his seat in one corner of the main room. Soon the people gathered, a large company.

"How I'd like to preach to them," mused Mr. Cartwright to himself, feeling quite out of place and more of a stranger than he had felt traveling the road alone. *I know what I'll do*, his thoughts resolved, *I'll stay here over tomorrow, the Sabbath day, and ask for the privilege of preaching to them all.*

He had hardly settled this point in his mind when a beautiful, sparkling young lady walked gracefully up to him and dropped a handsome curtsy right before his eyes.

"Sir," she invited pleasantly, and with winning smiles, "would it please you to take this dance with me?"

For a moment the preacher was in doubt of his own thoughts or feelings, so utterly unexpected was the situation. Then, impulsively, he decided on a desperate experiment.

"Why, I believe I will, thank you," he said as composedly as was possible, "that is, if you can put up with my clumsiness."

He rose as gracefully as he could, and the two walked onto the floor. The whole company seemed pleased with the young lady because of this act of politeness, shown as it was to a stranger. The fiddler, a colored man, plucked the strings of his instrument to assure its perfect tune for this special dance.

"Hold a minute, my brother," Mr. Cartwright addressed the fiddler. "For several years it has been my practice not to undertake any matter of importance without first asking the blessing of God upon it, and I now desire to ask the blessing of God upon this beautiful young lady and this whole company who have shown such an act of politeness to a total stranger. Let us all kneel down and pray."

Down went the speaker on his knees and commenced praying with all the power of soul and body he could command.

The young lady stood beside him in amazement for a moment. Then she fell on her knees. Others did the same, while some stood to their feet, some fled, and some sat still.

"Lord a mercy!" shrieked the fiddler as he ran off into the kitchen. "What de matter? What is dat mean?"

Sobs and cries for mercy rose in increasing crescendo

On and on prayed the preacher while sobs and cries for mercy rose in increasing crescendo all about him. The young lady who had invited him to dance lay prostrate on the floor by this time, calling desperately on the Lord to have pity on her poor lost soul.

At length Mr. Cartwright rose to his feet, gave timely exhortations to the penitent, and sang a hymn. Still, the moaning and crying continued. All night the preacher exhorted, sang, and prayed. By morning, fifteen of the company professed religion. All that day and the next night the meeting went on, until finally the number converted totaled more than thirty. A society was forthwith organized, thirty-two were taken into the church, and the host was appointed leader. A preacher was later sent to the group, and the revival spread until it touched all that region. Ironically, several of the young men converted at this dance became flaming evangels of the Gospel of Jesus Christ.

Mr. Cartwright never reflected upon this experience in later life without a sense of astonishment. He realized fully the miraculous power of the Lord in bringing his impulsive action to success.

"In some conditions of society, I should have failed," he confessed later. "In others, I should have been mobbed; in still others, I should have been considered a lunatic. But I concluded that if I failed, it would be no disgrace, and if I succeeded, it would be a fulfillment of the commanded duty to be 'instant in season and out of season.' At any rate, I reasoned I would have the satisfaction of taking the devil by surprise, as he has often served me."

Taking the devil by surprise must have been a choice specialty with Peter Cartwright, judging from the frequency with which he resorted to this expediency in his adventuring for God.

And it usually worked!

During the Nashville Conference, held in October, 1818, Mr. Cartwright was appointed to preach in the Methodist Church on Monday evening. It was a fashionable church, and Brother Mac, the pastor, had warned Mr. Cartwright to behave himself as he didn't want any exhibition of his eccentricities in the presence of his refined congregation. The circuit rider promised to do his best.

When the hour arrived, the church was filled to overflowing. Many were standing for lack of seating room. After singing and prayer, Mr. Cartwright rose to his feet.

"What shall it profit a man if he gain the whole world and lose his own soul?" he quoted solemnly, and then paused.

At that moment a trimly dressed army officer walked up the aisle, and finding no vacant seats, he stood, very gracefully leaning against the middle post.

"Pst! Pst!" a loud whisper from behind Mr. Cartwright warned, while his coat was being tugged at nervously by Brother Mac. "Be careful! General Jackson has just come in! General Jackson has come in!"

"General Jackson?" boomed Mr. Cartwright so all the audience could hear, a flash of indignation possessing his being like an electric shock. "Who is General Jackson? If he doesn't get his soul converted, he will be lost in hell as quick as a Guinea negro!"

The church pastor ducked his head, and tried to hide behind the pulpit, but the congregation, General Jackson included, smiled, then laughed outright.

"You're a man after my own heart, Mr. Cartwright," said the General heartily, when he met the daring preacher outside his hotel the next morning. "I am very much surprised that Mr. Mac should think I would be offended at you. No, sir. I approve of your independence. A minister of Jesus Christ ought to love everybody and fear no mortal man. If I had a few such independent, fearless officers as you are, and a well-drilled army, I could take old England."

Peter Cartwright never had the privilege of helping General Jackson "take old England," but he indeed had a conspicuous part in "taking" primitive America — for the Lord.

Equipped with a hardy horse, a library consisting of Bible, hymnbook, and discipline, and with a text that never wore out nor grew stale — "Behold the Lamb of God, that taketh away the sin of the world" — he went through storms of wind, hail, snow and rain. He climbed hills and mountains, zigzagged valleys, plunged through swamps, swam swollen streams, lay out all night, wet, weary and hungry, holding his horse by the bridle or tying him to a limb, slept with his saddle blanket for a bed, his saddle or saddlebags for a pillow, and his big old coat or blanket, if he had any, for a covering. Year after year he pushed from fort to fort, from camp to camp, from tent to tent, from cabin to cabin, with or without road or path. He shared the hardships and privations of the early settlers, accepting dirt floors for carpets, sitting on stools or benches for chairs, eating on split-log slabs for tables, using forked sticks and pocket or butcher knives, for knives and forks, and sleeping on bear, deer or buffalo skins before the fire, or sometimes on the ground in the open air.

Whatever the exigency, the Lord never failed to come to Peter Cartwright's rescue. At one time he started from home to attend four or five quarterly meetings, being District Superintendent at the time. He had traveled some eighty miles when a "most tremendous" rain fell. The whole face of the earth, where it was level, was a sheet of water. The ravines and little rivulets were swollen into large creeks. He still had thirty-six miles to travel to reach his meeting. He was told that it would be almost certain suicide to attempt to go on, as there was no road nor path for twenty miles, and no house nor cabin in that distance. The danger of being lost on the prairies was imminent, so the temptation not to attempt the journey was overwhelming. But when Mr. Cartwright paused a few moments, weighing the matter in his mind, his old Methodist preacher motto came to memory — "Never retreat till you know certainly you can advance no further," — and immediately his purpose was unalterably fixed to go ahead.

At about three o'clock that afternoon, having made slow progress because of the flooded condition of the creeks, and the soft, deep mud underfoot, he came upon the only cabin he had seen all day. But there was no one at home. Peering into the distance, he saw, about fourteen miles away, a point of timber which he knew was not far from the place where he was to hold his first quarterly meeting, so he decided to make a hard push and go through yet that day.

He had not gone far, however, when he came to a large creek too turbulent to cross. He went upstream, hoping to find a better crossing, but here it had swollen and spread out at least two hundred yards on the level ground. He rode in, nevertheless, and proceeded cautiously about one third of the distance across. By this time his horse was nearly swimming.

"Too far to risk it," he finally conceded. "After all, 'prudence is the better part of valor.' I'll have to go back."

Having retreated to higher ground, he pursued the creek bank downstream in search of a tree fallen across the water, over which he could carry his things, then return and swim his horse, thus avoiding getting his traveling equipment wet. By the time he found a tree felled across the narrow part of the creek, it was nearly night, so he decided to retrace his steps to the cabin and ask lodging of the occupants, who, he felt sure, would be home by this time.

Back to the cabin went Mr. Cartwright, but still no one answered his knock.

"Home or not at home," he vowed, "In the providence of God, I'll lodge here tonight."

So down off his horse he got, opened the door of the cabin and walked in. Red coals which had been covered with ashes to keep fire in the absence of the family, were still burning.

"Surely they'll yet come home sometime tonight," Mr. Cartwright remarked to his horse as he went out to strip him of the luggage, feed him, and put him up for the night.

The traveler's next concern was that he himself might have something to eat. After stirring up the fire and adding more fuel, he peered into a small corner cupboard, made of clapboards, backwoods fashion. There, to his great joy, he found a pan of cornbread, nicely baked. In one corner of the wooden chimney hung some excellent dried venison. This he broiled over the fire, and enjoyed a hearty meal.

The family still not having returned, Mr. Cartwright crawled into their bed which was nice and clean, and slept unusually sound all night. The next morning he arose early, fed his horse, prepared his breakfast much after the manner of his supper the night before, and saddled his horse. Before mounting, however, he knelt down on the doorstep of the cabin. With his broad-brimmed hat in one hand and his horse's bridle reins in the other, he lifted his face heavenward.

"God of the wayfaring, the homeless, the lonely," he prayed brokenly. "Accept the sincere thanks of thy child, so dependent and so needy, for thy providential care and thy most boundless mercy."

He paused in some moments of speechless worship and then rose to go on his way shouting and happy.

Just as God provided for Peter Cartwright this bounteous table in the wilderness, so he "thoroughly furnished" him "unto every good work" by giving him the resourcefulness, fervor and dauntlessness necessary to match the rough-hewn character of early America's pathless wilds and its pioneering people. In a true sense he was one of God's invincible "breaking plows." He rode preaching circuits in Kentucky, Tennessee, Indiana, Ohio, and Illinois, when the distances between appointments often stretched out to hundreds of miles, along which no guideposts except the sun and the evening star pointed the way. Because of the amazing strategies by which he outwitted gospel-fighters, dealt with difficult cases, and, more often than not, brought them to their knees, Peter Cartwright is remembered as the backwoods preacher unpredictable. But more than that, because of the shining road of salvation he blazed wherever he went, and the fire of glory he touched off in thousands of hearts by his self-less ministry, he is revered now, and evermore will be, as a saint beloved, a saint unforgettable.

Water From An Old Dry Well

"ANN, WHY DON'T YOU ask your Heavenly Father to send water in that old dry well and save us boys so much hard work?"

Henry had leaned back in his chair between mouthfuls of the delicious pot pie which no one but Ann could make so crunchy, so full of meaty goodness, so satisfying. The words had been spoken half-jestingly, yet when Henry saw that Ann had stopped her serving and seemed to be taking him in earnest, he went on.

"I was down in the well looking at it today. It's just as dry as the floor."

"Huh!" an older brother grunted disgustedly, "It'll not be anything else till fall rains set in. Not saying that isn't better than no well at all, but just when we need it worst every year, it plays out."

"Yeah," spoke up another languidly, "from June through September you can just count on not being able to count on it."

The others managed weary smiles over this brave attempt at humor, and left the table, work-worn, dusty and perspiring from the drudgery of the day, only to labor on till well after dark.

Each night the men and boys were late completing the chores because of endless trips by horse and wagon to haul water in barrels for the household and stock from the nearest well, one half mile distant. Each morning they were delayed in beginning the farm work for the same reason.

When they had gone, there passed again through Ann's mind the events of the supper hour. As the family had gathered around the table, she had been praising the Lord, as usual, and recounting the times He had so remarkably answered her prayers, not only in the past, but also that very day.

No one objected to Ann's spiritual reminiscences nor to her outbursts of praise. They knew full well that Ann enjoyed a strangely intimate relationship with the Lord, they knew she talked almost constantly with her Father as she went about her work, and they knew Ann's Heavenly Father talked to Ann, answering her prayers, both trivial and great, in His own mysterious ways.

Henry soon forgot his challenge, but Ann did not. That night when the work was all done, the lights out, the household asleep, Ann knelt in her room. She had taken Henry's words as a test not only to her faith, but to the faithfulness of her Lord.

"Now, Father," she reasoned, "You heard what Henry said tonight. If I get up in church and say, 'My God shall supply all your needs according to His riches in glory by Christ Jesus,' the boys won't believe I am what I profess to be if You don't send water in the well. They won't believe You are what You profess to be, if You don't send water in the well."

On and on she prayed that water might be sent, and finally, rising from her knees, she said, "Now, Father, if I am what I profess to be, and if Your Word is true, there will be water in the well in the morning."

When Ann entered the kitchen very early the next day, Henry was preparing to go after water. Ann picked up the two buckets and, as though she had been in the habit of doing so, went to the well. In amusement, Henry watched from the kitchen window. Simple-minded soul was Ann. He felt sorry for his joking the night before. Ann hooked one pail to the windlass and began to lower it. It would hit the bottom with a hollow plunk. Hadn't he told her the well was as empty and dry as a last year's bean hull?

But, lo! even from his distance, Henry heard an unmistakable splash! Ann was laboring hard now to wind up the windlass again. Down went the second bucket, and slowly she wound it up. Presently she walked in the kitchen door and set down at Henry's feet two pails brimful of clear, sparkling water. The boy stood dumbfounded.

"Well, what do you say now?" Ann asked with a little triumphant note in her voice.

Henry shifted from one foot to the other and stammered surprisingly, "Well, why didn't you do that long ago, and have saved us all that work?"

Ann did not take offense at this. She knew Henry, boy-like, was only putting up a front to hide his astonishment. She knew, too, that no matter how unthankful his words seemed then, he would have occasion many a day following to be grateful to her and to her Heavenly Father for bringing the water out of the rock, so to speak.

What sort of person was this Ann, who by her simple faith and lowly walk with God, is better known throughout Christendom by the appellation, "Holy Ann" than by her real name?

Born of hard-working Irish parents who made no pretension to piety, Ann Preston, at an early age was "hired out" as a servant girl. This would not have happened to her quite so soon in life had she shown greater aptitude to letters, but her school education had begun and ended in little more than a week.

"Poor Ann," the teacher had lamented before the whole class, tapping Ann on the head significantly. "She can never learn anything."

With this the child had been sent home in disgrace.

Though Ann's early life was spent in indifferent, if not in actually wicked environment, God's providence in due time led her to a position in the household of a Christian woman who undertook to teach her the Lord's Prayer. At the outset, her teacher was shocked at the ignorance of the girl. She first read the entire passage to Ann. Then she said, "Now repeat it after me, 'Our Father which art in Heaven.'"

Ann took up the words like a parrot, "Now repeat it after me, 'Our Father which art in Heaven.'"

In spite of patient reiteration and explanation, the good woman's efforts failed to make the least impression on the girl's memory, and she quit in despair.

A few years later Ann was employed by a devout Methodist woman, a Mrs. McKay, who took her to a class meeting. Here she saw some people weeping and some praising God. She watched to see whether the crying was real or whether they were wetting their faces with their fingers. Ann hardly knew what to think of it all. In fact, she was so nearly disgusted that when Mrs. McKay asked her why she didn't want to go again, she said she felt out of place with nothing to say when everybody else was speaking and praying and weeping.

"But you too have some reasons to praise God," her mistress encouraged her. "Who gives you food to eat and raiment to wear?"

Ann remained silent, but she afterward confessed that she had sullenly said to herself, "I guess I work hard enough for them."

However, the next week she attended class meeting again, remembering nothing she heard except this text, "But thou, when thou prayest, enter into thy closet, and when thou hast shut the door, pray to thy Father which is in secret; and thy Father which seeth in secret shall reward thee openly."

Ann did just that. After the day's work was done, she made her way to the attic, and scarcely knowing what was the matter, she wept and prayed, oblivious of all who heard her, until at twelve o'clock that night she saw the Saviour as He was on Calvary, and knew right then that His blood atoned for her sins. When she testified to her new-found experience, she said, "I felt something burning in my heart."

So changed was Ann's life after this and so devotedly did she live that her piety was known for miles around. It was not always venerated, however. While some held her acquaintance-ship in awe and reverence; more, perhaps, looked upon her in derision. One day a group of mocking boys scribbled in chalk upon her door, "Holy Ann lives here. Go in and have a word of prayer."

So well did the title fit that Ann's friends gradually began to call her by this new name given in derision.

Ann was nonplussed. She fled to her closet in the greatest humility.

"Oh, Father," she cried simply, "they're calling me 'Holy Ann.' Make me holy, so that the children will not be telling lies."

Her feeling of unworthiness to be called such a name caused her with all her heart to desire to fulfill the command of God, "Be ye holy, for I am holy." It affected the whole tenor of her life and wherever she went she became a faithful, fearless wit-ness for God and an inspiration to all who knew her.

Sometime after her conversion, employment in the family of a Dr. Reid who moved from Ireland to Canada, brought Ann also to these shores, where she spent the rest of her days, still in deep devotion to her Lord.

There were to be times, even in her adult life, when Ann would spend hours going over the words of a single Bible promise trying to memorize it so that she could quote it in class meeting, but to no avail. When she would ask her Heavenly Father why she could not remember the words, she always received the promise, "When the time comes, I will give it to you, so you need not worry." And He did.

If a passage or verse seemed to elude her memory just at the time she wished to quote it, she would stop in her testimony and say aloud, "Father, please give me that verse." And in the next instant, she would exclaim, "Oh, I have got it! Thank You, Father." Then she would repeat it perfectly.

Her acquaintances were amazed time and again when Ann quoted Scripture as the necessity arose, aptly appropriate to the occasion. Who could doubt that such a person was living in constant communion with her Lord?

Just as Ann's mind was blank in the matter of memorizing, so it was in the matter of her trying to read. Her desire to read God's Word started with her conversion.

"Oh, Lord," she prayed, "You took away this awful burden in my heart, intolerable to bear; now would You enable me to read one of these little things?" putting her finger on a verse.

God answered her prayer, and for the first time in her life, Ann was able to read. Through the years she learned to read the Bible easily, and even read it fluently aloud, but she was never able to read any other book or printed matter.

On one occasion, a newspaper was placed before her. She struggled hard to decipher some of the smallest words but to no avail.

"That seems . . . to be . . . 'lord,'" she finally faltered, pointing with her finger to a word in the news, "but I don't think it is my Lord. No, it can't be. My heart doesn't burn when I see it."

The word Ann was referring to was contained in a report of the South African War, telling of Lord Roberts' achievements.

No one ever had reason to doubt the genuineness of Ann's relationship to God. She conversed as freely with her Heavenly Father as she did with those of her household. And it was no wonder, for she spent more time talking with Him than with any human being.

A friend who slept with her one night told how, long after they had retired, Ann lay quietly communing with her Father, breaking out into praise from time to time, until nearly midnight. About five o'clock in the morning she awoke as usual, praising God, and arose. Since it was long before sunup, she groped in the dark for her clothes, but was unable to locate them.

"Father," she asked simply, "where are my clothes?"

At once she went to the place where she had laid them and picked them up.

"Thank You, Father," she said gratefully.

She then poured water into her bowl and began to wash. Suddenly she stood still, her wash cloth in hand.

"What is that You say, Father?" she questioned. Then in a moment she burst out joyfully, "Yes, that is it. Thank You, Father," and repeated the scripture she had read many times before — "Then will I sprinkle clean water upon you, and ye shall be clean: from all your filthiness, and from all your idols, will I cleanse you. A new heart also will I give you, and a new spirit

will I put within you: and I will take away the stony heart out of
your flesh, and I will give you an heart of flesh. And I will put
my spirit within you, and cause you to walk in my statutes, and
ye shall keep my judgments, and do them."

After washing and dressing, she knelt in quiet prayer for at
least an hour.

At one home in which she lived, the boys of the family
built a wee prayer home for Ann in the midst of a little grove of
cedar trees, near the back of the farm. Daily, Ann stole to this
quiet retreat and poured out her soul to God in impassioned
intercession for at least two hours. No other explanation need
be sought for Ann's secret of power with God. And no one can
measure the blessing that came down upon the lives of those
for whom she prayed because of her abandonment to this ministry.

Her prayers for the sick and unconverted were remarkably
answered, as multitudes could testify. People believed in her
and sent for her to intercede for them. Even the everyday trivi-
alities were all shared with her Heavenly Father in prayer. If
she or other members of the household lost articles of clothing,
toys or tools, she would lift her eyes to her Father, asking Him
to show her where they were, then she would instantly walk to
the spot where they were invariably found.

At one time after a long illness, when Ann was having a
difficult time getting around on her crutches, special services
were started in the church. Of course, Ann sought to get to meeting on every occasion, for she was ever anxious to assist in
prayer and lead souls to Christ. Imagine her dismay, then,
to awaken one morning, and see that a heavy snowfall had taken
place during the night.

"Oh, Father," she pleaded at once, "I can't go to meeting
tonight unless You send me help. You see how awkward I
would be in this snow on my old crutches. Won't You please
tell someone to make a path for me?"

At that time there was no man in the house, and the building stood nearly a quarter of a mile back from the traveled road.
On previous occasions in answer to her prayers, God sent a
neighbor or friend to shovel snow, but not today.

However, as Ann went about her work, peacefully confident
that God would answer her prayer, she was suddenly puzzled
to hear the girls shrieking with laughter.

"Oh, come quick!" they called to the rest of the family,
"Come see what is making the path for Ann today!"

Ann was one of the first at the window. And there they

The horses were galloping up and down in playful colt fashion

were — her path makers — horses, five in all, galloping up and down the lane in playful colt fashion, breaking a beaten path as straight as a line all through the deep snow. Four times they repeated their antics, making a path smooth and easily followed. As soon as they got out on the road, they scattered, but they had done their work in the lane well, and Ann had no difficulty getting to church that night where she told with beaming face how God had opened her way through the snow.

Surely, all that is meant by the phrases, "walking with God," and "talking with God," was illustrated most visibly, practically and constantly by this little woman so ignorant in worldly wisdom, but so learned in the things not of this earth.

As water flowed in the old dry well, so living water to bless a multitude of souls flowed from an ignorant Irish woman's heart. In a singular way, God took "nothing" and made of it "something" on which to hang a hallowed influence.

On June 21, 1906, as soon as it was known that Holy Ann, at the age of ninety-six, had passed away, hundreds thronged the home, anxious to get a last glimpse of the loved face. On the following Sunday the mayor of Toronto, Canada, testified in his church, "I have had two honors this week. It has been my privilege to have an interview with the President of the United States. This is a great honor. Then I have been pallbearer to Holy Ann. Of the two honors, I prize the latter most."

What tributes to an ignorant servant woman, unassuming, yet worldwide in her spiritual influence, whom God enabled to live a life exhibiting true, burning, genuine religion in everyday homespun!

"Ever, Only, All For Thee"

"Dear Frances, why not come," Marie softly pled with her sister, "and read with your feet comfortably warm before the fire?"

But Frances declined. "You see, Marie," she answered sweetly, "I could not then rule my lines neatly; just see what a find I've got! If one only searches, there are such extraordinary things in the Bible!"

"There are such extraordinary things in the Bible," Frances said.

So there she sat at her little study table by the window, shafts of sunlight turning her hair to spun gold, the curls clustering about her face and neck, her countenance radiant in the work of her King. Around her were collected pencils and paper, her Bible, a Hebrew Bible, Greek Testament, lexicons and an American typewriter.

To those of us who sing the songs of Frances Ridley Havergal, and read her unexcelled little books, it is almost unbelievable that she is dead. If she is, she indeed "yet speaketh." And every half hour we spend with her warm, intimate pen mes-

sages leaves us with the feeling that we have just enjoyed a
most inspiring chat in the heavenlies with a living personality.

Born at Astley, England, in 1836, the daughter of a distinguished minister of the Episcopal Church, Frances attracted
attention at a very early age, not only because of her fairylike
beauty and bright expression, but also because of her precocity.
At the age of three she was able to read and was often found
hiding under the table with some absorbing story. Until she was
six years of age she seems to have had no definite religious ideas,
but from that time until she was eight, she wavered between
solemn times of realizing her own lack of God, and periods of
trying to escape the kindly efforts of loved ones and friends to
talk with her about her soul's needs. At such seasons a chapter
in the Bible dragged out as a terrible bore to her. Any cut or
bruise (and she received many in those reckless days of wall-
vaulting and tree-climbing) was immediately magnified as a
reason why she could not possibly kneel down.

However, at the age of eight, one springtime morning, she
cried, "Oh, if God would make me a Christian before summer
comes."

From this time on, she seemed to be more steady in her
quest for a true Christian experience. When only eleven years
old she wrote:

> Oh! had I the wings of a dove,
> Soon, soon would I be at my rest;
> I would fly to the Saviour I love,
> And there would I lie on His breast.

Nevertheless, her faith for salvation did not completely take
hold until she had entered her fifteenth year. One evening as
she confided to Miss Cook, an older friend, about her longing
to know her sins forgiven, the light broke in upon her, making
the twilight glow with celestial beauty around her.

"Why cannot you trust yourself to your Saviour at once?"
Miss Cook asked. "Supposing that now, at this moment, Christ
were to come in the clouds of heaven, and take up His redeemed,
could you not trust Him? Would not His call, His promise, be
enough for you? Could you not commit your soul to Him, to
your Saviour, Jesus?"

A flash of hope dawned in Frances' heart. For a moment
she sat on the edge of her chair breathless. Her heart pounded
wonderingly. "I could, surely," she dared to whisper, as though
treading on holy ground.

Suddenly she left her friend and ran away upstairs to think it out. She flung herself on her knees in her room and tried to fathom this new hope that was becoming a reality in her heart. Then and there she committed her soul to the Saviour, not without some fear and trembling, perhaps, but she did, and earth and heaven were bright from that moment. She did truly trust the Lord Jesus.

The reality of Frances' new-found victory was proved in innumerable instances throughout the remainder of her life. When almost sixteen, she went with her parents to Germany. She stood alone as a Christian in the midst of one hundred and ten fellow students. Enmity to any Christian profession glowered in the very atmosphere, but Frances, never daunted, witnessed sweetly for the Master. Though she herself doubted that she had done any good among the students, eternity alone will reveal the truth. It is significant that toward the end of the school term, the students discontinued their small persecutions of her and some became even affectionate. She had "nailed her colors to the mast," as she expressed it, and had considered the whole experience to have been a "bracing" one.

The remainder of Frances' life was fraught with many ills which she took most patiently from the hand of her Master, though her frailty kept her from engaging in many public ministrations in which she would have participated otherwise. Perhaps if she could have been busy publicly, we today would be deprived of the many songs and books which she wrote while thus "hemmed in," although often she was denied even this form of witnessing for her Lord.

It would have taken a strong constitution to meet all the demands placed upon her. To a friend she described her incessant activity. ". . . fifteen to twenty letters to write every morning, proofs to correct, editors waiting for articles, poems and music I cannot touch, American publishers clamouring for poems or *any* manuscripts, four Bible readings or classes weekly, many anxious ones waiting for help, a mission week coming, and other work after that. And my doctor says my physique is too weak to balance the nerves and brain, and that I ought not to touch a pen."

Frances possessed unusual talent for singing and playing the piano, and was invited to sing often in gatherings, even at the Philharmonic. But there came a time, several months before she wrote:

Take my lips and let me sing,
Always, only, for my King,

when she made the choice of singing sacred music *only*. From that time forth, no matter what the nature of the gathering, she sang for Jesus.

Once while visiting in Ireland, Frances sang to a group of school girls. One of them described her as flashing into the room, caroling like a bird.

"She was like a burst of sunshine, like a hillside breeze," said the girl, "her fair sunny curls falling around her shoulders, her bright eyes dancing, and her fresh, sweet voice ringing through the room."

Many of the girls that day felt there must be the "music of God's own love in that fair singer's heart" which made at least one of them cry heavenward, "Lord, teach me, even me, to know and love Thee too."

On another occasion while visiting in Leamington, Frances attended an assembly at which many who love this world were present. She was asked to sing, and selected the song, "Whom Having Not Seen, I Love." Everyone seemed astonished, especially some Christian girls who had begun to think music could not be for the King's service.

Similarly, at a large gathering in London, she sang "for Jesus" in a spirit that revealed she enjoyed "the secret of His presence." It brought upon the company a dead silence. Later, a young man, a stranger to Frances, evidently impressed with her charm and sweet voice opened conversation with her. He was soon surprised, however, to find that she was quite easily drifting him from the playful banter with which he started, into a serious talk about his personal soul-danger and his only hope for safety.

The ease with which Frances turned her conversation with others into spiritual channels was surprising even to herself. She always attributed the gift to an endowment from the Master.

"I don't think anyone can say I force the subject," she wrote, "It just all develops one thing out of another, quite naturally, till very soon they find themselves face to face with eternal things, and the Lord Jesus can be freely 'lifted up' before them. I could not *contrive* a conversation thus."

No, nor did she take the credit for her talent in writing her hymns and little books. She claimed the Lord gave them to her line by line, and unless He did give them to her, she did not write.

At one time while traveling by train she had a curious musical vision. It seems that she heard strange and beautiful chords, generally full, slow and grand, succeeding each other in the most interesting sequences.

Said she, "I do not invent them, I could not. They pass before my mind, and I only listen. The chords seem to fold over each other and die away down into music of infinite softness, and then they unfold and open out, as if great curtains were being withdrawn one after another, widening the view, till, with a gathering power and intensity and fullness, it seems as if the very skies were being opened out before one, and a sort of great blaze and glory of music, such as my outward ears never heard, gradually swells out in perfectly sublime splendor. At one time I seemed to hear depths and heights of sound beyond the scale which human ears can receive, keen, far-up octaves, like vividly twinkling starlight of music, and mighty slow vibrations of gigantic strings going down into grand thunders of depths, octaves below anything otherwise appreciable as musical notes."

As we sing such songs as "Take My Life and Let It Be," "I Gave My Life For Thee," "Lord, Speak To Me," "True-Hearted, Whole-Hearted," we easily concede that they were inspired by the blessed Holy Ghost.

The consecration hymn, "Take My Life and Let It Be," had its origin in a little five-day visit which Frances made. There were ten persons in the house where she stayed. Some of these were unconverted and long prayed for, some converted but not rejoicing Christians. Instantly, her heart rose to God with the prayer, "Lord, give me all in this house."

And He did!

Before she left the house to return home, everyone had taken new ground in the spiritual life. The last night of her visit, Frances was too happy to sleep, and she passed most of the night renewing her consecration. All the while she was thus rejoicing, little couplets of song were forming themselves in her mind, and chimed themselves in her heart one after another till they finished with "Ever, Only All for Thee." No wonder we sing her songs feeling that they were directly inspired from above.

The same is true as we read her little spiritual gems, "My King," "Royal Invitation," "Royal Commandments," "Kept for the

Master's Use," and many other books, as well as poems. Each statement from her pen is scriptural, with a desire which stretches out into a yearning to help the reader find the place of complete abandonment to Jesus and the blessedness that follows.

Her writings are conversational, the tone of them making one feel that Frances herself has just dropped in for one of her heart-warming talks about the things of Jesus. Her words still live and throb and pulsate because they are Spirit-inspired and because to Frances they were more than theoretical platitudes, they constituted her own very life.

Particularly during the seven years before her death Frances felt that she had more definitely entered into all the will of God, and was living out in everyday life each couplet of her Consecration Hymn, beginning with, "Take my life and let it be, consecrated, Lord, to Thee."

At this time, the words, "Take my silver and my gold — not a mite would I withhold," were revealed to her as meaning not only the money that came into her hands, but also her jewelry. She joyfully slipped off her ornaments, gathered together fifty-three pieces in all, including a jewel cabinet, gold pencils, brooches, and some massive chains given her for literary toil, and shipped them off to London to the Church Missionary Society. Thus disposing of them, she sent the money, about fifty pounds, to missionary work in India. Said she, "I never packaged a box with so much pleasure."

Frances' many exploits for the Lord no doubt shortened her stay on earth, but she was always ready, even happy and eager in the thought of going to be with her Lord. This desire was fulfilled when she was only forty-two years of age. A little prayer her mother had taught her, Frances had made her own life-prayer, "Oh, Lord, prepare me for all Thou art preparing for me." Her prayer was answered for she had meant it when she penned the last couplet of her Consecration Hymn:

> Take myself and I will be
> Ever, only, all for Thee.

Suffering the Loss of All Things

DAVID SAT CROSS-LEGGED in the shade of the fruit trees and vines that overspread his African hut. His day had been anything but satisfying. And he was completely worn out.

"Tired as a stone," he sighed. And then, addressing nothing in particular, "Wonderful evening."

He threaded a needle. Strange how he had not foreseen all the trifling tasks that would be his when he came out alone as a missionary doctor. All his morning he had spent with the hordes of children who followed him as though he were the Pied Piper of Hamlin. Intriguing little scamps they were. One couldn't just dismiss them with a wave of the hand. So he had taught them songs and told them Bible stories. A woman could have done better with them, he knew.

Then in that scorching afternoon heat he had washed his sheets, towels and clothing. Now, after cooking his own supper and putting the dishes away, he was sewing on buttons and patching the knees of his trousers. In just a little while he must conduct the regular evening gospel service.

Anticipating this, his heartbeat quickened with the passion of a missionary! Ah! Preaching the Gospel was his meat and drink! Perhaps, after all, he should have listened to those motherly advisors who had urged him to marry before coming to the field. If there were someone to look after the house and its duties — someone to teach the children, to nurse his patients, he could spend more time reaching out with the Good News to those hundreds of villages from whose huts he had seen the smoke rising while he was yet dreaming back in England.

Still, he had been blissfully free from family responsibilities the three years he had been in Africa. More than that he had never seen a girl yet who came up to his code of qualifications. Daughters of missionaries had miserably contracted minds, he thought, and Colonial ladies were worse. Besides, he was too busy to think of anything of the kind.

39

The next morning David was up early. Verdant hillsides were massed in a multicolored semicircle behind the village. Pushing off its misty bedtime covers, the sun reached with delicate fingers into the lovely valley of Mabotsa and made it a shimmering fairyland. Here the missionary joined his black-skinned neighbors in the task of digging canals for their gardens.

This morning there was excitement in the group.

"Doctor!" the Bakhatla chief exclaimed when David appeared, "There are lions in the hills! Their roars thundered all the night! Watch! Don't leave hut when sun goes down!"

David had heard the terrifying racket in the night. Once before the lions had been on a rampage and had even leaped among the herds in the open day, killing some cows. Fear gripped the tribesmen that the same thing would happen again.

"We are bewitched," they said, "whoever saw the lion, the lord of the night, kill cattle by day? They do it once, they not stop to do it twice."

Sure enough, before the day was over a lion, roaring with rage, sprang among the sheep huddled on the hill opposite the missionary's hut and slew nine in broad daylight.

"Come!" ordered David, "if we get the leader, the rest will leave!"

He ran for his gun.

The natives trembled at the thought of trying to kill the fearful beast, yet they were ashamed not to follow their leader. Soon the Bakhatla warriors, bristling with spears, closed around the little tree-covered hill where the lions were crouched. David and a native schoolmaster, named Mebalwe, waited with guns.

"There he is!" choked Mebalwe. As he spoke, he fired.

The bullet struck the rock on which the beast was sitting and he bit at the spot as a dog bites at a stick thrown at him. Then leaping through the circle of men, he bounded off unscathed. Two more lions followed. The natives were spellbound. Not one threw a spear.

"No use," one of them said with conviction, "we're bewitched."

The circle broke and each one headed for home. For the missionary, however, the hunt was not over. Going around the hill, he spotted one of the beasts sitting on a rock behind a small bush.

David shot quickly and surely. Nothing happened. The next instant, another bullet hit its mark.

"He's shot! He's shot!" yelled the black men.

"Stop!" shouted David. "Keep back! I'll load again."

He rammed another bullet into his gun, but before he could aim, terrifying screams tore through the tenseness.

"Run, Doctor — he's on you!"

In another moment David and the lion fell to earth together in a sickening thud. Again the natives screamed but were powerless to help. Amid the deep angry growls of the lion they heard bones being crunched to splinters. Then the beast shook his prey as a terrier does a rat.

Two more shots split the air!

David shot quickly and surely

Mebalwe had fired his gun, but missed. Now the lion turned on him. With tail erected in rage, and a mighty lunge, he bit Mebalwe's thigh. By this time, a man whose life David had saved previously, ventured near enough to aim his spear. Suddenly the lion turned and leaped upon his shoulder, but then, just as suddenly and unexpectedly he fell, a victim, finally, of the shots David had given him.

With eleven tooth marks in his flesh, and his shoulder bone excruciatingly torn, David could think of only one thing to do. He would go to the home of the nearest missionaries — one hundred fifty miles south — at a place called Kuruman. He had met Robert and Mary Moffat in England before sailing for Africa, and now in his pain and distress, his heart turned to them.

A fortnight of weary travel brought David to the station of the Moffats, but no white friends were there to greet him.

"Teacher go to England," he was informed by the spokesman of the tribe. "He's on way back now. Almost here."

After questioning the black men more specifically, David found the report to be true. Robert Moffat and his family had already landed at Cape Town and were slowly making their way north to Kuruman by oxcart. He decided to meet them. After one hundred fifty miles more travel southward he came upon the party. Glad greetings were exchanged and then David told of his misfortune.

Strangely enough, however, the dreadful experience which had tortured him for nearly a month now, suddenly paled before a new experience — a sweet, restful one. For even while he talked with Mr. Moffat, he stole numerous glances sidewise to meet the large brown eyes of young Mary sitting on the oxcart seat beside her mother, and found the sight to be quite a pleasing one. That night he dreamed of the sweet, sunburned face, the charming manners. Perhaps missionaries' daughters were not so undesirable, after all.

During the weeks following, Mother Moffat carefully watched over her patient, and was gratified to see him gradually recover. It was on a certain enchanted evening during this time that a very wonderful thing happened. David and Mary had spent various evenings sitting beneath the almond tree a little way from the mission hut, and had found each other's company quite agreeable indeed. But this evening was different. A sacred hush surrounded their happiness. David was in a quiet mood. His thoughts raced back to the end of another day when he had sat cross-legged before his hut in Mabotsa with a needle in his hand. Now in his mind, the hut faded away, and in its place, the picture of a little brick and stone house merged into clearness. In a low rocker under the fruit trees and vines sat Mary, sewing on buttons and patches. Presently, the hordes of eager children who used to clamor for his songs and Bible stories came into view, and there again was Mary, taking them under her wing and into her heart.

"Mary," David's voice was low and gentle, "Mary, I need you."

There was a pause as he searched her face.

"I need you, immeasurably, but . . . if this were not true, my love for you is such that I would be constrained to ask you this question anyway. Would you, could you so much as consider becoming Mrs. David Livingstone?"

For a moment all was silence. The almond tree leaves bent to listen and the evening held its breath.

Mary's eyes shone with a new, warm light. Oh, she did love this brave young pioneer missionary! And David's voice was not the only one that had spoken. God had been showing her a duty to be performed, a place to fill.

"I will, David . . . yes, I will," she breathed softly, "and under God I'll try to be a real missionary as well as the wife of David Livingstone."

David had found his heart at last. Before the year closed, the wedding took place, and she who bore the honored name of Moffat, exchanged it for one, little known at the time, but soon to be famous throughout the whole earth.

For several years the two consecrated young people worked together, evangelizing one tribe, then moving on to another. But when the hardships of travel proved too much for the babies God had sent into their home, David decided that Mary must take them to England and he would go on alone.

"Suffering the loss of all things . . ." David said simply as he tenderly kissed his Mary good-by.

"Yes," she returned, with the radiance of supernatural courage lighting her countenance, "for the excellency of the knowledge of Christ Jesus my Lord."

Each felt that no matter at what expense of separation and suffering, David must open up the dark continent to the Gospel. Their sacrifice was not in vain.

After thirty years of unwearied effort to evangelize the native races, to explore the undiscovered secrets of this benighted land, to abolish the desolating slave trade of Central Africa, David finally set out on his last journey. It has been most generally regarded as another journey of exploration with the purpose of finding the source of the River Nile. Deep in Livingstone's heart, however, lay a greater, a supreme purpose — that of gathering information which would enable him, upon his return to England, to strike one mighty blow at the slave trade.

Said he, "If the good Lord permits me to put a stop to the enormous evils of the slave trade, I shall not grudge my hunger and toils. The Nile sources are valuable to me only as a means of enabling me to open my mouth with power among men."

He set out with high hopes and determination but it was not long until his native friends saw that he could not last the journey through. When Livingstone became too weak to walk, he was carried on the shoulders of his faithful blacks. Then one day his debility would not permit even this.

"Susi," he said to one of his devoted servants, "lay me down for a bit — here in the shade. I can go no further."

Seeing that their master's weakness would require more than just a short rest, the natives hastily constructed a rude hut, and laid him in it. Tenderly they watched over their beloved missionary. Then night came on. Not wishing to rob his faithful ones of their sleep, Livingstone called Susi to him.

"Light my candle, Susi," he said, "then all of you can go and rest. Only tell Majwara to stay close by in case I should need him."

The candle was lighted and one by one the natives retired. Only Majwara, a mere boy, lingered behind. He lay quietly at Livingstone's door but not to rest. The long night wore on, Majwara heard no sound within the hut, no call from his master, but somehow he could not feel that all was well. In the wee hours of the darkness, he left the hut door, and crept to the side of his sleeping companions.

"Susi! Chumah!" he whispered hoarsely, "There must be something wrong with Master. I am afraid."

The three hurried into the hut. The light was still dimly burning and in its flickering shadows they saw their beloved missionary kneeling as in prayer by the side of his cot, his face buried in his hands.

They tapped him lightly on the shoulder and spoke his name. But there was no response. Again they called him. But there was no answer.

"He's gone!" whispered Susi in awe, and the others nodded.

There was no time to lose. Amid choking sobs which alone broke the solemn hush of that memorable night, Susi, Chumah, and three others embalmed the body of David Livingstone, having buried his heart in African soil. Soon, they set off with the mortal remains of their master, and journeyed amid terrible dangers many, many weary miles to the coast, whence the body was taken to England and buried in Westminster Abbey among the noted of the world.

Livingstone traveled over thirty thousand miles through the heart of Africa. Many of these journeys took him where no other white man had ever been. Everywhere he went he opposed slavery and all the other evils he found to be so prevalent in this heathen land.

Among his last written words were, "May Heaven's rich blessing come down on everyone, American, English or Turk, who will help to heal this open sore of the world."

Thus, David Livingstone, and Mary his helpmeet, will always be remembered among the most heroic souls of earth, and many there be, who, throughout eternity, will rise up and call them blessed — blessed because they suffered the loss of all things for the excellency of the knowledge of Christ Jesus their Lord.

Not With a Sigh But With a Song

THE JOY OF MARY'S HOMECOMING had not been without its anxiety. The five-year period of toil as a missionary in the *zenanas* of India had not satisfied itself with ordinary wages.

Mary was ill.

She did not know how often the members of her family had stolen scrutinizing glances at the transparent whiteness of her face, and had looked away again with the sickening apprehension of their hearts intensified. Doctors admitted their bewilderment. Even the Cincinnati specialists had not concealed their perplexity. They had treated Mary, operated, and now, after several months of attempted diagnosis, had all but come to the point of conceding their helplessness either to determine the nature of her disease or to cure it.

"One more trip," they had requested. And Mary went.

The verdict that was finally given the young missionary was not altogether a surprise, for there had lurked in Mary's heart a nameless terror, a terror she had not dared to countenance. Now it could be ignored no longer. She was a leper! The only outward signs of her malady were a strange spot on one cheek near the ear, and a constant tingling pain in the forefinger of her right hand, but her doom was unmistakable.

Mary Reed staggered into the street and wended her way through the crowds, scarcely knowing what she was doing or where she was going, and . . . caring less. "Oh, if only the Lord had told me I was going to die tonight," she gasped through dry lips, "I would have said, 'Thy will be done.' But this . . ."

Then in a flash she was shown the purpose of it all. In her mind's eye she was carried back again to India, where, because of ill health, she had been sent to Pithoragarh, high in the bracing climate of the Himalayas, for rest and recuperation. The few weeks she had spent there were filled with earnest preparation for the ministry immediately awaiting her at Cawnpore, but in addition to her language study, she had observed missionary

46

work among the lepers. Envigorated physically, Mary had returned from Pithoragarh to four years of successful labor at Cawnpore, thence to a year of teaching in the Girl's Boarding School at Gonda. But it was no doubt at Pithoragarh that she had contracted the disease that was now wasting her body.

Mary's sensitive, refined nature recoiled from memories of five hundred hopeless, repulsive creatures doomed to a living death, thrown on the rubbish heap of exile, loathed by mankind. But now, being a leper herself, she could minister effectively to the leper! It was all as plain as day. The poor, unwanted creatures of Pithoragarh were to be, in the providence of God, the sheep of her flock, her "little ones," as she later often called them, or, as frequently, "Christ's little ones."

The evening of Mary's return from Cincinnati to her home was exquisite in its coloring. Never had the sunset outlined the low-lying hills of southeastern Ohio with more gorgeous beauty, nor etched the maples in silhouettes more lacy. A soul less brave than Mary would have given up the thought of continued missionary work, and would have settled down to what life she had left amid the quiet joys of such home surroundings.

The little front gate's latch clicked behind her, and with the click, Mary the inimitable put behind her the shock her journey had inflicted. With radiant face and the old triumphant lilt in her voice, she announced to her family that she would return to India soon.

The few days that followed vibrated with the excitement, the rush, and the sharing in Mary's anticipation of resuming her chosen task. For, though the separation would mean sacrifice sore and costly, not one of this consecrated family would keep God's handmaiden from her life's mission. The evening before her departure might well be the last evening that the family circle would be unbroken, they knew. Mingled emotions filled each breast.

"Just let me go tomorrow without a special good-by," Mary pleaded unexpectedly, "as though I were returning for supper. Will you? It will make it so much easier for me."

And each one in the home smiled his or her agreement to play the curious game, little knowing that instead of a game, a grave reality had laid the foundation for Mary's clever request, and that she had chosen to forego the exchange of farewell kisses lest she contaminate with leprosy the dear ones she would leave behind.

The next day Mary tripped down the path, through the little

gate whose latch clicked behind her, and was soon on the train that would take her to New York. Gaily and lovingly she waved farewell, while her family tearfully stood on the station platform. A dramatic moment indeed.

Stopping by at the home of a friend in London, Mary's consecration and calm faith in the wisdom of God once more sweetly verified itself. When her friend suggested that every Christian ought to unite in prayer for her recovery, Mary's only response was, "I have not yet received any assurance of healing; perhaps I can serve my Father better thus."

On her last evening in London she sang,

> Straight to my home above
> I travel calmly on,
> And sing in life or death,
> "My Lord, Thy will be done."

And with the Christlike resolve that her affliction should not hinder her usefulness, but rather that she should triumph

Mary looked out at Chandag Heights, in the Himalaya Mountains

over it, she made her way back to India, alone, yet assuredly not alone, and as she herself said, "under conditions in which no other missionary ever returned." It was not until she reached Bombay that she wrote to her mother the truth of her condition.

"Chandag Heights, the beautiful, in the Himalaya Mountains," is the address from which Mary Reed dated her letters after arriving at her post of duty among the lepers. Here is her description of the place in her own words:

> Away to the north, seemingly only two or three days' journey, are the eternal snows whose grandeur and sublimity

are indescribable; they are so pure and bright and peace-suggestive! At sunset and sunrise it is easy to imagine them visible foundations of the Eternal City, they are lighted up with such a halo of glory. But it is of the mountains among which I live that I want to tell you. They enclose a lovely valley called Shor, like a massive and exquisitively beautiful frame around a magnificent picture. My home is on the crest of the range which forms the western boundary of the valley, or the left side of the picture frame. And the picture! A rich and beautiful valley, containing about six square miles, lies more than one thousand feet below my lofty and lovely "retreat," and is dotted with numerous villages which are surrounded by clumps of trees and terraced green fields of rice, wheat and other grains. Through this valley a little river and its tributaries wind in and out, and a ridge of low hills divides it.

Contrasting this with the sultry slums of an eastern city to which she might have been assigned, no wonder Mary rejoiced in the pure atmosphere of her home on the heights.

Her arrival awakened feelings among the lepers, which, if recorded, would be of pathetic interest. Having walked up from Pithora, which was her temporary home until her bungalow could be built at Chandag, she told, in a short service she held with the lepers, how she had been set apart by God to minister to them. Deeply touched by this revelation of the self-sacrifice of their new friend, they seemed to forget their own affliction in their loving sympathy for hers, and tears ran freely.

Some time after she had begun her ministry of love at Chandag Heights, the Rev. G. M. Bulloch, of the London Missionary Society visited her work. He found Mary busy in the hospital, tending three patients in a much advanced stage of leprosy. She was binding up with her own hands the terrible wounds, and speaking soothing words of comfort to these poor distressed ones. He was surprised to see her so active and cheerful.

"I've never felt better," Mary smiled, "and was never so happy in service."

There was a time when Mary had written from Chandag, "The disease made decided progress for six months after my arrival at this mountain retreat, and I suffered intense pain most of the time. But I found His grace sufficient. . . . Words are empty to tell of a love like His. He has enabled me to say, not with a sigh, but with a song, 'Thy will be done.' "

The subsequent improvement noticed by Dr. Bulloch, both in her physical and mental status was not the result of medical treatment, for she had given up all such under a strong sense that God only required of her faith in Him and in His healing power. She felt that this affliction was in the line of the divine will for her. As from God's hand she had received it, so now in God's hand she left it.

After less than eight years at her post, and practically single-handed, Mary developed the institution under her charge from a mere collection of huts and stables, in which some thirty-seven lepers were housed, to an establishment with an average of eighty-five or ninety patients, sheltered in convenient houses specially built for them. This involved surmounting legal obstacles to obtain additional land, the supervision of native workmen, the arranging of various building contracts, and the control of the finances, as well as meeting the food requirements of her large and growing family. All of this, to say nothing of the spiritual, moral, and medical supervision of the hopeless and oftentimes helpless beings around her, could have been accomplished only by a dauntless soul strengthened by divine help in answer to daily prayer.

Strange as it may seem, the symptoms of Mary's disease gradually decreased, and finally, after ten or twelve years, they completely vanished. She was healed! But did she take this as a welcome opportunity to flee her vile surroundings? No, the lepers had responded quickly to her love and sacrifice. Here was her life's calling. And here she remained, her work of mercy expanding-continually.

For fifty-two years Mary Reed was superintendent of the leper homes. Her own little abode she named "Sunny Crest Cottage." When, in later years, a biographer was given her reluctant consent to write a book telling of her life and labors, what was Mary's horror but to find that beneath a photo of her little dwellingplace they had printed the caption, "Mary Reed's Lonely Home."

"No," she firmly objected. "The book must not go out carrying such a statement. Recall every copy, and change the title to read, 'Mary Reed's *Lovely* Home.' Not one moment in this little abode has been lonely, for *Jesus* has been with me *all* the time!"

Indeed, she had gone to this little home in the beginning, not with a sigh, but with a song.

Pilgrim's Journey to Heaven

JOHN STRODE HOPEFULLY into the little town of Bedford, England. His tall form, swinging vigorously into each forward step, his intelligent countenance, even his wavy hair combed lightly by the fingers of the morning breeze, all spoke of the purpose pounding in his breast — that of finding more pots and pans to be mended so that the baby and her mother back in his Elstow home could be provided for.

No one would have guessed the poignant heartache that intensified his purpose, for John was not the kind to wear his feelings on his sleeve. But there it was, just the same. Baby Mary had been born blind! So much the more dependent then was she upon his utmost care, and so much the more was his love kindled for her.

At first John had been resentful, stunned to think that God had allowed such affliction to descend upon his home. But the mother's quiet resignation, her sweet trust in the goodness of God, and above all, her amazing prayer for John himself, had served to tame somewhat his always too fiery spirit.

"Dear God," she had said, "help this poor husband of mine! He is more sightless far than Mary!"

And strange though it sometimes seemed, John had almost begun to think she was right! Surely she would have to concede, though, that he was not as blind as when she had married him. That startling denunciation of Sabbath desecration presented by Preacher Hall some months before had cured him of his tip-cat games on the Lord's Day. And not only had he quit the games, he had discontinued also his ringing of the bells for the games.

John experienced a pleasant tinge of self-satisfaction in this thought — a satisfaction which vanished, however, almost as quickly as it had come, for, quite against his will, he was forced to remember, too, how helpless he was to shake off the night-

51

mare of fear that seized him now whenever he so much as entered the steeple-house. Foolish it was, he knew, seeing that he was there, not to ring the bells, but only to look on while another did it. This reasoning, nevertheless, served not to change the reality.

The minute he had entered the door lately, he had been seized with a horrible thought. "How if one of the bells should fall?" The awful words had kept ringing, ringing in his ears in perfect time with the tolling of the bells. With that, he had decided to stand under the "main-beam that lay athwart the steeple, from side to side, thinking here he might be safe." But again he had been tortured with the possibility that should the bell fall with a swing, it might first hit the wall, and then, rebounding upon him, kill him in spite of the beam. After this he had ventured no farther than the steeple door where he felt quite safe. For, he thought, if now a bell should fall, he could slip out behind the thick walls and escape with his life notwithstanding. Today, as he thought about it, even this assurance suddenly slipped and lost its footing. *What if the steeple itself should fall?*

This was a problem too hard to be solved and one that left John limp with fear.

In the midst of such strange and muddled considerations, John rounded a corner and entered a familiar lane in Bedford town. Shafts of golden sunlight paved the grassy way with bright patterns of shimmering glory. Birds sprinkled their cheery songs upon the pure, free air of the new morning, and John felt as though his mind was suddenly cleansed and his heart renewed. Down the roadway loitered neighbors and friends passing the time of day. Closer at hand sat three aged women on a doorstep. John slowed his pace a bit, if haply thereby he might discover the topic of their conversation, for even he would not think of being so rude as to interrupt some serious discussion to ask for pots and pans to mend.

Just then he caught a word, two words, which told him plainly that the women were discoursing upon the things of God.

". . . born again!" one had said with joy. Then she continued, "My Lord has given to me, even me, all things richly to enjoy!"

" 'Tis true," said another, "and His promises greatly refresh, comfort, and support us against all temptations of the *Evil One*."

John halted, and would have turned to go the other way, so mean and unworthy in his soul did he to himself appear. But then he reminded himself, "I, too, have been favored of the Lord and may I not converse with these as one acquainted with the doings of the Almighty? Has not His hand been upon me since the day that I was born? When I was but a boy did He not pluck me out of the creek of the sea, and rescue me from drowning? And when I fell from the boat in Bedford River did not His mercy yet again preserve me? And what less can I say about the time I walked in the fields with my companions and an adder crossed my path? When, having stunned it by striking it over the back with my stick, I forced open its mouth and plucked its sting out with my fingers, if God had not overshadowed me with tender care, I might, by my foolhardiness, have brought myself to an early end. Likewise, in the army, His providence sought me out. I was called out with others to besiege a point, but just before I left, one of the others desired to go in my place and as he stood sentinel where I would have been, he was shot in the head with a musket-bullet and died."

John had stopped now, feigning a readjustment of the bag he had thrown over his shoulder for the pots and pans he hoped to mend.

"Besides," his reverie continued, "haven't I gone to church e'en twice a Sunday ever since my pretty wife started reading the books her father gave her on our wedding day? Though we had not so much beside as a dish or spoon between us, yet 'The Plain Man's Pathway to Heaven,' has been worth more than all, I trow. Yes, and 'The Practice of Piety,' has shown this man what he'll have to do to get to heaven. In fact, I've reformed tremendously already . . ."

He paused, as the scenes of a recent day flashed vividly across his memory. He had been standing at a neighbor's shop window, cursing and swearing in a manner that had become almost second nature, when lo! the woman of the house who had heard him from within, suddenly appeared at the doorway. John knew her as a very loose and ungodly wretch, but this day her eyes had snapped with the fire of a kind of protest foreign to her usual temper.

"John Bunyan," she had almost screamed, "You swear and curse at such a fearful rate, I tremble when I hear you! You're the ungodliest fellow for swearing I've ever heard in all my life! Shame on you! You're enough to spoil all the youth in the whole town if they but get near you!"

John hung his head even now in secret shame at the remembrance of such a reproof from a woman as wicked or more so than he. It was futile, he had thought then, to try to reform, so much a part of him the awful habit had become. But, wonder of wonders! and he understood not how it had come to pass, from that time forward he had never uttered an oath.

Indeed, God had done great things for him. He had quit ringing the bells, or even going near (he now suddenly vowed); he had started going to church; he had quit swearing . . . why, surely he was eligible to enter into conversation with the women on the doorstep. He too could talk "briskly" in matters of religion.

John Bunyan ventured into the company of the saints sitting in the sun. But he soon found that their talk was far above his reach. Indeed they were quite beyond his understanding. They discoursed as people who had found a new world — as those who dwelt alone, apart, and were not to be reckoned among their neighbors. John soon saw the wretchedness of his own heart. He saw, as the women disclosed their former state, that his own righteousness was filthy and insufficient to merit him a home in heaven. He saw that he must needs be born again, that his sin was not only in his deeds but in what he actually was inside. He saw that what he needed was not only to have his sins forgiven, but to have the heart that wanted to sin, cleansed.

Young Bunyan went home that day with a spirit greatly subdued. He had seen something that called him irresistibly from the earthly to the heavenly. And, from then on, it became as difficult for him to take his mind from heaven to earth, as it had been previously to get it from earth to heaven. There developed just one obsession in his life: to know the God of just men made perfect, and the way to the Celestial City where He dwells.

Then and there, John began reading the Bible in earnest. And one day a strange word gripped his heart. "I will cleanse their blood that I have not cleansed . . ." spoke the Lord through his prophet Joel.

Ah! thought the reader, *It sounds most surely like the very thing I need — a cleansing of my blood!*

He went back to the three women and told them all his

heart. They, in turn, related his case to Mr. Gifford, pastor of the village church, who neither stopped nor rested until he had hunted John down for God.

About this time, John, with his frail, pretty wife, little blind Mary, and three younger babes, moved to Bedford, where they had the opportunity of attending Mr. Gifford's church. One Sunday morning as John listened to a sermon on the glorious text, "Now thanks be unto God which always causeth us to triumph in Christ!" unprecedented things happened. "Water stood" in his eyes, and he responded to the pastor's entreaty to sinners "to close with Christ."

It was the decision point in Bunyan's life. Though he came to know firsthand that the afflictions of the righteous are many, yet he proved too that the Lord delivereth him out of them all. In the same year that the family moved to Bedford, his precious wife died, leaving him to battle on alone with his little blind Mary, Elizabeth, John and Thomas, for four lonely years. Then God gave him Elizabeth, a capable wife, who fitted in as a mother overnight.

Spiritual struggles were John's also. Having been so great a sinner, he was plagued with many a doubt as to his being included in the company of the elect. And his soul cried out, "O Lord my God, call me also — even me!"

At one time, just as he found himself most hopeless of ever attaining eternal life, bright words fell with celestial sweetness upon his spirit. "Look," they said, "look at the generations of old and see: did ever any trust in the Lord and was confounded?"

At another time when harrassed by the thought that he had missed his chance of heaven, the Lord spoke gently, surely, "And yet there is room, my son, yet there is room!"

In this state of wavering between doubt and faith, young Bunyan wondered greatly to see old people hunting after the things of this life as though they were to live here always. "If they," said he, "so much labor after, and shed so many tears for, the things of this present life, how am I to be bemoaned, pitied and prayed for! My soul is dying; my soul is damning! Were my soul but in a good condition, and were I but sure of it, ah, how rich should I esteem myself, though blessed with but bread and water!"

To such a seeker, God could do no less than manifest Himself, and by many a scripture which Bunyan testifies did "spangle" in his eyes, assurance was granted him that, on the merits of the blood of Christ, he was indeed accepted of the Father.

From this time, John was aware of fire in his bosom, "such a secret pricking forward" to the ministry that he soon began to preach, and found to his surprise that "folks came in to hear the Word by hundreds, from all parts." He spoke to his avid hearers wherever and whenever they could get together. Revival spread through the countryside.

But John had no preacher's license. His ministry drew the crowds from the established churches of the State, and when Charles II came back to the throne in 1660, persecution began.

One day, just as John began to preach to his good people gathered in a wooded sanctuary in the country, officers roughly broke up the meeting and hauled the young preacher before the court magistrates, who in turn sentenced him to perpetual banishment. Just as quickly as that it all happened, and for no other offense than the "crime" of preaching the inescapable truths of the Gospel.

"But Father dear," little Mary sobbed, her sightless eyes brimming with tears, "you haven't done anything bad. Why, oh, why must you be kept in jail?"

This was John's heartbreak, his greatest cross. To be snatched from family and home, from pitiful little Mary especially, dearer because blind, to leave her unprotected, unprovided for — well, it was like tearing the flesh from his bones. The poor prison fare, the prison labor, the prison filth, all were nothing in comparison to this! Yet, by the grace of God, John was enabled very soon to write:

> The prison very sweet to me
> Hath been since I came here!
> And so would also hanging be
> If God would there appear!
>
> This jail to us is but a hill
> From whence we plainly see
> Beyond this world and take our fill
> Of things that lasting be!

Of course, God saw to it that a way was made whereby he could provide some sustenance for his wife and babes, poor though it was to be. Sitting, day after day, beneath the one tiny window in his lonely cell, John made thread-laces to sell that his family might have bread. And Mary, faithful child that she was, stood with him at the prison gate as he sold them.

Tauntingly the jailor offered him release. "And what would you do tomorrow," he tempted him, "if I let you go tonight?"

"Why, preach!" John answered staunchly. "Yes, I'd preach, to be sure. 'Woe is me,' said Paul, 'if I preach not the gospel,' and the same woe, forsooth, is upon my own soul!"

In the prison, John took up his pen to write

So, still in the prison John dwelt. His "home," he called it, since God did abide there too. For twelve long years the cruelty of men's hatred for God and His servants, held him in the solitude of Bedford jail. When the thread-laces were finished for each day, he preached to his companions in bonds — a congregation who could not get away — or took up his pen to write, or played sweet tunes to the praise of his Father above on a flute he had made out of his stool leg without spoiling it for its original purpose. It was during this time that he prepared for publication many religious works, particularly one, "Grace Abounding," in which he revealed the most intimately spiritual secrets of his soul.

Bunyan made the most of prison life and stedfastly held his faith in God. Sorrow seemed added to sorrow, however, when one day his precious Mary failed to meet him at the gate. He had feared for her lately. That cough and the transparent whiteness of her countenance had at times almost made his heart stand still. Could it be that the worst had come? Must he face the possibility that she would be forever torn from him?

Hardly had he breathed the thought, when, peering across old Bedford jail bridge for her familiar form, he caught sight of another, Elizabeth, clothed in mourning! Yes, it was true! Mary was dead! For six years, Mary had stood at the gate beside him.

It was well he could not know that now he would stand there six years more, a broken-hearted man, alone! His love for God and his belief in the goodness of the Almighty never wavered, even in this extremity, but it was many a day before he again had the heart to write a word!

When at length Bunyan was liberated from his dungeon, he become the pastor of the same little church of which the holy Mr. Gifford had been the shepherd. Crowds thronged the place, and so passionately did the divine fire burn, that mission stations sprang up all over the countryside. Even so, there were to be times when the bitter antagonism of the powers that be threw the worshipers out of their edifice. Nothing daunted, however, they met in a barn or an orchard, a dance hall or a cottage, a houseboat or on a street corner.

Bunyan's love for Christ only flourished in the fray. It became a fury within him, so much so that he wrote seven books in one year, aside from preaching. In all, he is said to have written during his lifetime more than a million words. Of his works, the most famous and best-loved is *The Pilgrim's Progress,* a spiritual allegory which has been translated into more than eighty languages. No book, except the Bible itself, has had greater influence for good on the mind of man than this one. Written in simple, straightforward English by a plain, straightforward man, this immortal story bids fair to be read as long as our literature endures. It illustrates the trials that beset a Christian on his way through life, and the characters are so human, one is instantly interested in each for his own sake, as well as anxious to know what happened to them all.

When Bunyan died in London in 1688 at the age of sixty, he had done more than all King Charles' bishops to turn the thoughts of the people of England to God. His holy influence has not been confined to England, however. John Bunyan belongs to the world. Our faith is strengthened because he was strong. We are encouraged to triumph in suffering because he endured as seeing Him who is invisible, and because he found His grace sufficient. We find our own love for the Master burning more warmly because there once lived a man to whom nothing else mattered but to exalt his Christ, a man lost in love for Jesus.

More Like an Angel Than a Man

JOHN FLETCHER LAID DOWN the letter, and pulled his chair up to the breakfast table.

"My tea, please," he addressed the maid.

Tapping his fingers nervously on the cloth-covered board, he immediately lost himself in pondering this disconcerting missive from his home town in Switzerland, which the postman had just delivered. For disconcerting it was!

He was well aware that his parents disapproved of his going into the army. But this venture of his was not "going into the army" in the strict sense of the word. He merely had accepted a captain's commission and had engaged to serve the King of Portugal on board a man-of-war which was at that moment making ready with all speed to sail out of Lisbon's harbor to Brazil. The money he had asked his parents to send he had not intended merely for himself. He had felt sure he could invest it to "vast advantage" in this new country to which he was going, and his parents as well as he would profit greatly thereby.

But they had refused.

Well, he would proceed anyway. He had no doubt that his parents' objection was based on their belief that he ought to give himself to the ministry. He had believed the same thing intermittently since he was seven years old. But though he would never so much as entertain the thought of fighting against a call of God, he felt now that the prospect of preaching the Gospel could never be his. Why, he was miserably lacking in the state of heart commensurate to a minister of the Gospel! Definitely unqualified for so high and holy a calling!

At this moment the maid approached with the teakettle, and John was recalled from his disturbing reflection. She was hurrying. He was glad of that! For if he did not soon betake himself to the wharf, the boat would be off without him!

"Here," he offered politely, holding his cup so that the pouring could be more quickly dispatched.

But just at that instant the teakettle slipped from the servant's hands, and a seething swash of boiling hot water scalded the young man's leg from his hip to his toe!

Just as quickly as that were the plans of the youth dashed to pieces, and he was in bed days on end bemoaning his lot! But when, in due time, he learned that the ship on which he was to have sailed perished at sea, his thoughts took a different turn. Why, just why, had his life thus been mercifully saved again?

For this was not the first time John Fletcher had been miraculously preserved from almost certain death. While fencing with his brother when just a lad, he had received an abdominal wound so deep that he carried the scar to his grave; again he fell from a wall so high that death would have been his certain plight had he not providentially landed in a quantity of freshly-mixed mortar; three times he had nearly drowned, once having been pinned under a building for twenty minutes. Of this latter experience, John Wesley remarked later, "Some will say, 'Why this was a miracle!' Undoubtedly it was. It was not a natural event, but a work wrought above the power of nature, probably by the ministry of angels."

Baffled as he now was in every attempt to become a soldier, John gave up his aspirations in that field. Having then no business to engage him, he made his way to London, here to study the English language. Later he was to serve as tutor in the household of a Mr. Hill at Ternhall, Shropshire.

All this time, John had the fear of God deeply rooted in his heart, but there was no one to take him by the hand and lead him forward in the things of the Spirit. Indeed, being naturally one of genteel behavior, and eminently sweet-tempered, he had never become aware of his own inward heart need until one Sunday evening when a servant entered his room to replenish his fire. John was writing music in preparation for the next day's duties in the classroom.

"Sir," said the servant with kindly but serious concern, "I am sorry to see you so employed on the Lord's Day."

John made no answer, though at first his pride had risen in indignation and resentment that he should have been reprimanded by a servant. Then upon reflection he realized that the reproof had been just. So he immediately put away his music, to become a strict observer of the Lord's Day from that very hour.

He was ever known to aspire after rectitude, and as being anxious to possess every moral perfection. Such a soul God did not leave to grope in darkness very long. When Mr. Hill went to London to attend the Parliament, he took his family and the young tutor with him. While they stopped at St. Albans, John walked out into the town and did not return until the others had set out again for London. A horse had been left for him, however, and he overtook the party in the evening.

"We waited for you as long as we dared," apologized Mr. Hill. "Was it anything serious that detained you?"

"Nothing serious, no," John returned, "and I regret my causing you concern. But as I was walking, I met with a poor woman, who talked so sweetly of Jesus Christ, that I knew not how the time passed away."

"So?" queried Mrs. Hill pleasantly, then continued, "I shall wonder if our tutor does not turn Methodist by and by."

"Methodist, madam?" questioned John vaguely. "What is that?"

"Why," replied she, "the Methodists are a people that do nothing but pray; they are praying all day and all night."

"Are they?" exclaimed John. "Then by the help of God, I will find them out, if they be above ground."

He did find them out not long afterward, and was admitted into the society. Encouraged and inspired by these people of God, John soon entered into the experimental knowledge of salvation for which his heart had so long hungered. From this time his hopes and fears, his desires and pursuits, were totally changed. He walked cheerfully as well as valiantly in the ways of God, taking up his cross daily.

It was not long after John Fletcher "felt the powers of the world to come" that he found within his being an earnest longing —

> To pluck poor brands out of the fire,
> To snatch them from the verge of hell.

Thus, even a considerable time before he was admitted into holy orders, he began exhorting sinners to righteousness with such unspeakably tender affection that multitudes were drawn to hear him. And by the blessing of God his words made so deep an impression on their hearts that very few went away empty.

In 1757, John Fletcher dedicated himself to the work of the holy ministry.

He continued in London assisting John and Charles Wesley, and preaching wherever he had a call, then in 1760 was given the vicarage of Madeley. Here he was to stand forth as a preacher of righteousness and as a burning and shining light for the next twenty-five years.

Entering upon his ministry with an extraordinary degree of earnestness and zeal, he instructed the ignorant, reasoned with gainsayers, exhorted the immoral and rebuked the obstinate. He had a most resolute courage in reproving evil. It is well known that to daring sinners, he was a "son of thunder." In season, out of season, he diligently performed the work of an evangelist. He spoke as in the presence of God, and taught as one having "divine authority." Said one, "Without aiming at sublimity, he was truly sublime; his . . . word soared on eagles' flight above humanity. In short, his preaching was apostolic."

Like the vigilant pastor he was, he daily acquainted himself with the needs of the people, anxiously watching over their households, and diligently teaching them from family to family. Esteeming no man too mean, too ignorant, or too profane to merit his affectionate attention, he condescended to the lowest and most unworthy of his flock, cheerfully becoming the servant of all.

If a knock came at his door, though in the depth of the coldest winter night, his window was thrown open in a moment. As soon as he learned that someone had been hurt in a mine pit or that a neighbor was near death, he hastened to the suffering one without any thought for the darkness of the night or the sharpness of the cold.

John took a bell in his hand and set out at five o'clock every Sunday morning

When some excused themselves from attending the services by saying that they could not awaken early enough to get their families ready, John Fletcher himself took a bell in his hand and set out at five o'clock every Sunday morning. On foot he made his rounds, even to the most distant points of his parish, inviting all the inhabitants to the house of God.

His heart went out to other sheep also. To a little society which he had gathered about six miles from Madeley, he preached two or three times a week, beginning at five in the morning. And for many years he preached regularly at places eight, ten, or sixteen miles away, returning the same night, though he seldom reached home before one or two in the morning.

The parish of Madeley being of some size, it abounded with people who, either through infirmity or misfortune, were reduced to a state of poverty and distress. Over this despised and destitute part of his flock Fletcher watched with unusual solicitude. Not content with offering them the consolations of the Gospel, he contributed largely to the relief of their temporal needs, and divided among them the greater part of his income. The profusion of his charity constantly emptied his purse, frequently unfurnished his house, and sometimes left him destitute of the most common essentials of life.

Once a poor, God-fearing man fell into great difficulty. Fletcher's heart went out to him at once. He took down all the pewter from the kitchen shelves and thrust it into the man's arms. "Here, take this," he insisted, "It will help you, and I can do without it; a wooden trencher will serve me just as well."

It was no wonder then that Fletcher's selfless ministry, to which he gave himself early and late, in foul weather and fair, in heat and cold, rain and snow aggravated his tendency toward a "consumptive disorder" which he had battled for some time. His weakened constitution was still more seriously impaired by his intense and uninterrupted studies and writing, over which he pored at times for fourteen, fifteen or sixteen hours a day, almost without intermission, allowing himself only a little bread and cheese or fruit, two or three times in twenty-four hours. Then sometimes being too absorbed in his work to stop even long enough for these light refreshments, he would merely take a drink of milk and write on again.

From Fletcher's pen came many valuable works on controversial and spiritual subjects, but the toll was paid in a complete break of health which kept him on the brink of eternity for the remaining fourteen years of his life.

Said he, when he began to realize the precariousness of his physical condition, "O how life goes! I walked, now I gallop into eternity. The bowl of life goes rapidly down the steep hill of time. Let us be wise: embrace we Jesus and the resurrection. Let us trim our lamps, and continue to give ourselves to Him that bought us, till we can do it without reserve."

In the latter end of this same year, he said to Charles Wesley, "Old age comes faster upon me than upon you. I am already so gray-headed that I wrote to my brother to know if I am not fifty-six instead of forty-six."

Thinking that a change of air and climate might benefit his health, Fletcher made several excursions to the continent. On one occasion as he was passing through southern France, he expressed a longing desire to visit the Protestants in the Sevennes Mountains, whose fathers had suffered so greatly in the cause of godliness. Though the journey proved long and difficult, yet he could not be prevailed upon to give up his resolution to attempt it on foot.

Said he to a friend, "Shall I make a visit on horseback and at ease, to those poor cottagers, whose fathers were hunted along yonder rocks like partridges along the mountains? No. In order to secure a more friendly reception among them, I will visit them under the plainest appearance, and with my staff in my hand."

So thoroughly did he make himself a blessing and inspiration to one family under whose roof he spent the night, that the villager told the story to his neighbor the next day. "And to think," he concluded almost fearfully, "I nearly refused to take a stranger into my house — a stranger more like an angel than a man!"

While traveling through a part of Italy, Fletcher directed the driver to stop before he entered upon the Appian Way. He then ordered the chaise door to be opened, assuring his fellow-traveler that his heart would not permit him to ride over that ground upon which the Apostle Paul had formerly walked, chained to a soldier because he had preached the everlasting Gospel.

As soon then as Fletcher set his foot upon this old Roman road, he took off his hat, and walking on with his eyes lifted up to heaven, returned thanks to God in a most fervent manner for that light, those truths, and that influence of the Holy Spirit which had continued to that time because of the apostle's faithfulness.

In his home town of Nyon, Switzerland, Fletcher preached many times to multitudes who flocked from all quarters to hear him. Among others, a good old minister past seventy years of age heard him gladly, and earnestly entreated him to lengthen out his visit to their village that they might hear more of the glorious Gospel from his lips. When the old man found that his desire could not conveniently be granted, he wept unashamedly. Turning to Fletcher's fellow-traveler, he exclaimed, "O sir, how unfortunate for this country! During my day it has produced but one angel of a man, and it is our lot to be deprived of *him!*"

Recovering his health to some degree while in Switzerland, Fletcher used his strength as fast as he gained it, and the stronger he became the oftener he preached. His ministry, however, was not confined to the churches. Upon one of his morning walks, he saw a great crowd gathered at the door of a house.

"What does this mean?" he asked a bystander.

"Why," was the reply, "a poor woman and her babe lie dying within."

Fletcher made his way through the curious number to the bedside of the stricken. Death, indeed, appeared to be very near. The minister of God addressed the people standing about concerning the imminence of eternity, the need of a Saviour, and His sufficiency for the soul's need. Said he, "He is able to save you all from sin, as well as to save this mother and infant from death. Come, let us ask Him to save both us and them."

While Fletcher prayed as only he could pray, the child's convulsions ceased, and the mother received healing and strength. The people were utterly amazed. They stood speechless, almost senseless! When they finally came to themselves, the man of God was gone.

"Who could it have been?" they asked one another incredulously.

There was a general shaking of heads. No one knew. Then a voice ventured, hushed and reverent, "Certainly, my friends, it was no man. Certainly . . . it was an angel!"

In all his travels, including several itineraries in company with John Wesley, Fletcher missed no opportunity of buying up proper occasions to speak of heavenly things.

Visiting at times Lady Huntingdon's Seminary at Trevecca, to whose superintendency the Countess had appointed him, his challenges to holy living so inspired the students that he was loved and revered like Elijah in the schools of the prophets. His whole conversation was in heaven. The result was that his listeners seldom hearkened long before they were all in tears, and every heart had caught fire from the flame that burned in his soul.

He was indeed a pilgrim in this world. So much so that he was unallured by its smiles, unmoved by its frowns. While thousands and ten thousands were contending around him for the advantages and honors of the present life, he desired to pass unnoticed through its "idle hurry," without being entangled in its concerns or encumbered with its gifts. Considering one thing only as absolutely necessary to his happiness, he pursued the substance, rejecting the shadow.

As death approached in his fifty-sixth year, Fletcher's silent meditations were frequently accompanied with so much visible delight, such an ecstatic glow diffused itself over his whole countenance, and his eye was directed upward with a look of such inexpressible sweetness, that one would almost have supposed him to be conversing with angelic spirits about his approaching entrance into heaven and the glory that should follow.

Once in particular the man of God was so filled with the love of the Most High that he could contain no more, but cried out, "O my God, withhold Thy hand, or the vessel will burst." But he afterward told a friend he was afraid he had grieved the Spirit of God, and that he ought rather to have "prayed that the Lord would have enlarged the vessel, or have suffered it to break, that the soul might have had no further bar or interruption to its enjoyment of the Supreme Good."

Perhaps remembering this, he continually admonished his brethren at Madeley to seek the fullness of the pure love of God in their hearts. Said he, "Let not a drop satisfy you: *desire an ocean!*"

It was just such an ocean that from the heart of John Fletcher overflowed to water the thirsty ground wherever he went and made him the seraphic minister of Jesus Christ he was. It must have been for this that God had miraculously pulled him from the jaws of death so many times, and to make of him a man after His own heart — yet indeed, as the French peasant had aptly said, "more like an angel than a man!"

God's Warrior

FOR A BREATHLESS heart-stopping moment, the flimsy canvas of a much worn, one pole tent flapped crazily in a brisk breeze, then yielded itself to a crinkled resemblance of its intended contour, as William Booth and a few helpers gave a final tug at the ropes.

"Good enough!" shouted one. "At least it didn't rip going into shape!"

"Fasten it well," ordered the future general of the Salvation Army. "Looks as though the gale is rising, and the tent's survival is precarious in the best of weather."

The tent was pitched in the Quaker Burial Ground, just off Whitechapel Road in East London. Booth's observation having told him that only a small percentage of the people were being reached with the Gospel by the churches, he proposed to take the Gospel to them. And the tent, he hoped, would be a means to this end.

Every evening from six to seven, Booth and his co-workers conducted a rousing open air service on the street, then led those they had gathered about them in a singing procession to the tent, where in striking and electric language he asked them what they were going to do with Jesus.

The arrangement worked well for awhile. Then catastrophe fell. Mild atmospheric conditions gave way one week to London's more typical weather, namely, a downpour of honest British rains. First of all, generous drippings from holes in the tattered tent roof tended to wash the unsaved clear away. Then one evening a sudden squall completely flattened the cheap canvas covering.

At considerable expense Booth repaired the tent, only to find it sadly torn soon again. Through the rents the wind howled, damp and chilly. He and his little group, huddled together in common misery, courageously held services as long as they could, but were finally driven to find new quarters — in a large dancing room.

Neither the inclement aspect of one place, nor the incongruous situation of another daunted this intrepid searcher for souls. Because of the fire of God in his bones, Booth was to be found through the years to come, preaching wherever people would listen to him — in dancing saloons, stables, sheds adjacent to pig sties, from theater stages, circus rings, racecourse grandstands, footboards of railway carriages, ship-captain's bridges, African huts, street corners.

The tent episode was only the first of a thousand bouts with opposing forces that demonstrated the victory-or-die spirit of God's warrior, William Booth.

His heart bled for the masses in East London, so many of them without God and hope in the world, but eager to hear what he had to say. They were poverty-stricken and Booth could hardly expect from them sufficient financial support to sustain him. Nevertheless, his faith and that of his wife were equal to the venture. Thus, he had found a tent and started out.

Having commenced his ministry as a young man within the confines of the Methodist Church, he had withdrawn from this connection because of the restrictions they enforced upon his evangelistic outreach. This was in July, 1861. Booth was thirty-two years of age at the time, and already had a young family dependent upon him for support.

The idea of forming his followers into a really permanent organization came to their leader only gradually. However, his converts would not go to the cold, formal churches. Besides, Booth found he needed them to help him in his work. At first he named his group the East London Revival Society, then, the East London Christian Mission, later shortened to the Christian Mission, and finally changed to the Salvation Army — a power which spread like a prairie fire throughout the length and breadth of the United Kingdom.

His was a militant organization and it was rapidly disciplined. It had ranks, uniforms, and colors — blue, red and yellow — blazoned with the words, "Blood and Fire." When Booth, who naturally embodied the General of the movement, asked a soldier, "When will you be ready to go to Australia or Canada or Norway or Brazil?" the reply he wanted to hear was, "Tonight, General!" He felt that, like any soldier in the Queen's army, a Christian soldier's kit-bag should always be packed and ready for a forced and sudden march.

Booth's rules and regulations for members and officers allowed for no taint of the world. Following this line in their preaching, it was not uncommon for Salvation Army leaders in their services to see penitents lay their worldly adornment and other idols at the speaker's feet. Once, after the General's eldest son, Ballington, had uttered only a few words, seekers at the penitent form covered it with their trinkets — seven feathers, three pipes, three pairs of earrings, three brooches, two other fine pieces of dress jewelry, one grand pin, one Albert chain, one tobacco pouch, and two pieces of twist, one of which was twenty-four inches long!

Advancing against all kinds of sin, the Army encountered not only the opposition of the devil, but also the scorn, ridicule, and enmity of the people belonging to the respectable churches of the day. Like the Wesleyan Methodists before them, Salvation Army soldiers were everywhere assaulted and insulted. It was not uncommon for the Salvationists to end up with broken ankles and wrists. One had a piece bitten out of his arm. Another, on an inspection tour alone, had been pelted and mobbed for an hour and a half.

General Booth did not require of his soldiers what he himself was unwilling to suffer. The first march the General and Mrs. Booth made to Albert Hall in Sheffield ended in a riot. They, their officers and soldiers arrived at the Hall wounded, bleeding and battered, their clothes torn and covered with filth, their band instruments smashed. This was the story everywhere they went. Every available hall or room was often closed against them. Once, Booth wrote from Salisbury, "The evangelists have to get off the street and into houses to escape the mob. Police refuse protection. Nevertheless, there is a good society. A lot saved. We must not give up: we will not." The General's attitude in all storms, whether of the type that flattened his canvas tent or the kind instigated by heartless villains, was the same — "Go straight on!"

A certain church dignitary was asked what he thought of the Salvation Army, and the reply was, "Well, to tell you the truth, I don't like it at all; but to be candid with you, I believe God Almighty does."

The General never ran after earthly rulers, or showed any disposition to court their favor; but he said constantly, "Here we are; if any government, municipal or national, likes to use us, we can save them more than half of what they now spend upon their poor and criminal classes, and do for these far more than Christian government officials, however excellent, ever hope to do."

"Gentlemen," said a Town Councilor in a German city, "The Army can do for your poor what you can never attempt. You can deal with them from without. The Army works upon them from within, and produces results that will considerably lighten your burdens."

Thus, the frown of public opinion gradually gave way to the smile of favor.

As years passed, the warfare was not dependent upon the older folk alone. Many of the Army's leading officers were truly converted before they were ten years old, so that at thirty they were already veterans in the fight. The children of the Booths themselves were to be seen filling responsible places in the Army, most of them invading new territory on foreign soil, leading their troops to America, France, India, South Africa, New Zealand, Switzerland and finally to the ends of the earth.

The General had a way of inspiring his men and women as well as his family, to learn how to die. They did not shrink from his instructions, mainly because his instruction was backed by personal example. He was always telling his family, his soldiers, all England, to go and *do* something. He, himself, could not rest. "I am very tired," he wrote once, "but must on – on – on – I cannot stand still. I have worked today and lain down again when I could sit no longer, and then got up and gone on again. A 'fire' is in my bones . . ."

At one time in South Africa Booth talked for seven hours, so sorely did his heart yearn over the lost.

This concern for souls did not burst upon him merely when he appeared before the public. It possessed him night and day, well or ill. One evening in later years, Bramwell stopped by the General's home to bid his father good night. It was later than usual, and Bramwell found the old warrior pacing up and down impatiently.

"General," Bramwell exclaimed, "What are you doing up at this hour? You should have been in bed long ago!"

His father looked up quickly. "Bramwell," he replied, "I'm thinking! Thinking!"

"What are you thinking about, General?"

"Ah! Bramwell," cried the aged prophet, throwing up his hands, "I'm thinking about the people's sin! What will the people do with their sin?"

"Ah!" cried the aged prophet, "I'm thinking of the people's sin! What will the people do with their sin?"

At the mere mention of sin, the old gentleman's brows would contract, his eyes flash, his tongue hiss.

"Sin!" he cried once to Commissioner Railton. "Sin is a real thing — a damnable thing. Sin is devilish. Sin! Go into the slums of the great cities — pick up little girls of six years of age sold into infamy by their parents; look at the drunken mother murdering her child, the father strapping his crippled son — sin! — that's what I call sin; something beastly and filthy and devilish and nasty — nasty, dreadfully nasty."

When the grim old man with ivory face, black, flashing eyes, tangle of white hair and beard, leaned over the rostrum and denounced sin, the people sat white and spellbound. They wept, they hung their heads with conviction, their bosoms heaved with emotion, they were convinced, convicted, and a multitude were converted. At one time there were no less than three thousand eyes brimming with tears.

He held that no man is safe, no man is at the top of his being, no man is fully conscious of life's tremendous greatness until the heart is definitely and rejoicingly given to God. He was like all the supreme saints of the world in this insistence upon the necessity for a cleansed heart and a will devoted to the glory of God. He believed that this message must be shouted, dinned, trumpeted, and drummed into the ears of the world before mankind can awaken to its truth.

Band music, processions, and demonstrations were used by the Army to attract the people. However, the keen sense with which the General always distinguished between the enjoyment of demonstration and of real fighting was strikingly manifested on one of the great Crystal Palace days. Looking down from the balcony upon the vast display, when some fifty thousand Salvationists were taking part in various celebrations, he noticed a comparatively small ring of their converted military and naval men kneeling together on the grass, evidently within hearing of one of the bandstands upon which one band after another was playing, according to program.

"Go and stop that band," said he to one of his A. D. C's. We must not have those praying men hindered in their fight for souls by the music."

. This was only one example of his frequent abandonment of any program or practice or arrangement which seemed to him to have only demonstrative effect, when any more enduring benefit could be otherwise secured.

When King Edward asked the General what his recreations were, Booth said, "Sir, some men have a passion for art, others have a passion for riches, I have a passion for souls."

His oft quoted slogan was, "Go for souls and go for the worst." This objective he continually set before the Army. His view was the same as the Saviour's own, that we owe to every man every care that a truly brotherly heart must needs bestow. And he made no difference between the rich, the poor, the great, the small. He neglected none because of their low estate. He feared not to be faithful to any because of their exalted position.

His absorption in the salvation of mankind made him unwilling, even if he had time, to participate in social pleasantries. He could not chatter, nor could he relax and let the world around him die. While people babbled in his presence, his impulse was to cry out, "Is it right with your soul?"

In an outburst of concern for the lost, he once exclaimed, "Oh, God, what can I say? Souls! Souls! Souls! My heart hungers for souls!"

It was this obsession that sent him on a "rampage" around the world, recovering the lost. Though approaching his eightieth year, his physical vigor seemed to abate not. In six motor tours he passed from end to end and from side to side of Great Britain, gathering crowds from day to day for six weeks at a time. By speaking to at least two large indoor meetings every day, and by meeting crowds of people gathered enroute and in the market squares, he could also speak to perhaps millions he had never before contacted.

Twice while touring America, once during McKinley's administration, and once during that of Theodore Roosevelt, Booth was invited to open the Senate with prayer. He talked for twenty minutes with President McKinley, "who quite endorsed the doctrine that without the grace of God in the heart, there was little hope of permanently reforming the people."

This was the beginning of many honors conferred upon the General by emperors and kings and presidents. But, although he appreciated them for his own sake and far more for the sake of the Army, his heart grew more lonely and his oppression by the world's wickedness more deep. His private sorrow, too, flooded his heart most sorely when his public honor was highest. For, added to the heartache occasioned by the death of his wife, came the shock of the sudden death of his second daughter, Emma, killed in a railroad accident. The General was left a lonely, heart-broken old man, but even now he did not falter. He wrote to Eva, one of his younger daughters, "I love God, and lay myself afresh at His feet, and for Jesus Christ's sake, I want to be saved from the sin of doubting Him. I shall go on . . . Precious Eva, we will go on — we must go on!"

When the end of life's journey drew near, bringing with it the loss of his eyesight, Booth still remained the grand old soldier the world knew him to be.

"God knows best," he said. "I have done what I could for God and the people with my eyes. Now I must do what I can for God and the people without my eyes."

This he did. He continued to speak, he continued to write as long as strength would permit.

"While women weep as they do now," he said, "I'll fight; while little children go hungry, as they do now, I'll fight; while men go to prison, in and out, in and out, as they do now, I'll fight; while there is a drunkard left, while there is a poor lost girl upon the streets, while there remains one dark soul without the light of God, I'll fight — I'll fight to the very end!"

Like Luther, his answer to all objections, worldly or unworldly, would have been, "I can no other."

Booth's influence extended to the two hemispheres, and, perhaps, as much among the savage as the civilized. The Salvation Army recruited millions of faithful ones in the most diverse nations. Nationally the Army has done magnificent work in fifty countries.

True, much of the General's work led in paths of social reform — soup and soap for the hungry and unkempt, beds for those who had nowhere to lay their heads, homes for fallen girls and orphan children, Thanksgiving and Christmas dinners for the needy, clothing for the poorly clad, all of which must have solicited from the Master the welcome words, "Inasmuch as ye have done it unto one of the least of these, ye have done it unto me," — but the major passion of his life was to see souls delivered from their sin, and this passion burned in his plans for a future even beyond his own life-span.

One who saw the aged General conducting a meeting said, "Then it seemed to me like a picture, as when a grey warrior, a commander with snow white beard and keen profile, stands upright by the mast of a ship and gazes straight before him toward a new country. And General Booth, despite his eighty-one years is looking out toward new land. He does not live on memories like the generality of old men. He does not allow himself any favored spot by the fireside. Full of fight and always leading, General Booth has plans for the future such as the youngest might have."

The world will long remember this warrior for God, William Booth, whose fight against sin and conquest of souls girdled the globe.

A Gale From Heaven

THE OLD RAIL FENCE bordering a woodland just north of Adams, New York, was warmed with golden fall sunshine one October morning in 1821, and its many ivy-sheltered angles would have tempted most wayfarers to stop and sit awhile in rest and meditation. But the presence whose shadow fell upon its solitude today hurried on. Usually serene and self-possessed, the young man proceeded nervously, with frequent glances backward toward the town. Indeed, he shrank within his coat and skulked along the fence to hide himself from the eye of the village, then plunged into the timber and its enveloping secrecy, only to scramble on for a full three quarters of a mile before he stopped.

The young man proceeded nervously

Perhaps now he was far enough away, he decided. And, too, here was a nook made by some large trees having fallen conveniently across one another leaving an open space between. This would afford him seclusion even more secretive.

As though he had hardly been able to wait for the opportunity, the young man immediately fell to his knees and re-

75

peated once more the words he had muttered continuously since his dash into the wood.

"I will give my heart to God before I ever come out again! I will give my heart to God before I ever come out again!"

A sly autumn zephyr stole through the almost gaunt tree-tops, listened a moment, then stirred the dry leaves on the ground into a mad scamper. The rustling roused the youth. He jumped to his feet. Surely someone was coming! And if he could help it, they would not catch him . . . *praying!* He glanced furtively in every direction. Unbelievably, no one was in sight. So once more he concentrated on his quest for God. But again it was not for long. Repeatedly, panic overtook him at the thought that someone would see him on his knees!

Then a new consideration seized him. It reined him up short! He must have a proud heart! That's what was wrong — a proud heart! It was a very disconcerting revelation, but one he could not evade. Why, it was this that was standing in his way to finding God — this wicked shame at the thought that a human being should see him on his knees before his Maker!

An overwhelming sense of his atrocity so possessed the youth that he cried out at the top of his voice in protest. "I will not leave this place," he exclaimed, "if all the men on earth and all the devils in hell surround me! What! such a degraded sinner as I am, on my knees confessing my sins to the great and only God, and ashamed to have any human being, and a sinner like myself, find me on my knees endeavoring to make my peace with my offended God! God forbid! God forbid!"

At that moment, a passage of scripture dropped into his heart with a great flood of light: "Then shall ye go and pray unto me, and I will hearken unto you. Then shall ye seek me and find me, when ye shall search for me with all your heart."

It was all he needed. God had spoken! He trusted in the veracity of the Most High, and fastened upon His Word with the grasp of a man about to drown. Promise after promise crowded into his soul and he took them every one as infallible truth, the assertions of God who could not lie.

At last his mind became so full and so transported that before he was aware of it, he had sprung to his feet and was tripping up the ascent toward the village road. Whether he was actually converted or not never so much as entered his mind. Brushing through the bushes about him and wading through the leaves beneath his feet, he resolved emphatically so that

all the world might know if it wanted to, "If I am ever converted, I will preach the Gospel!"

The most profound spiritual tranquillity enveloped him at
this moment. And though its mystery was overwhelming, yet the
repose of his mind was wordlessly sweet.

He returned to the village to find that he had spent a
whole morning in the woods. It was now noon, but he had no
appetite for earthly food. He went to his law office — the office
he was wont to enter with some pride, since his senior partner
had pulled down the sign from above the door which had read,
"Benjamin Wright, Esquire," and had put in its place a new
one announcing that here was the office of "Wright and Finney,
Attorneys at Law." Just now the squire was out. Young Finney
tuned his bass viol and, as he often did, began to play and sing
some hymn selections. But today found him different than afore-
time. He could not sing those sacred words now without being
overcome with weeping.

When the squire finally entered the office, the two associates moved their furniture to a new location as they had previously planned. As dusk fell, Finney built a good fire in the
open hearth hoping to spend the evening alone in prayer. In
due time, the books and furniture being adjusted to his satisfaction, Squire Wright bade his junior partner good night, and
went home. No sooner had the door closed upon his friend than
a great wave of glory seemed to melt Finney's soul into a
stream of liquid love for God. He rushed into the room back
of the front office, for pray he must!

No light, no fire cheered the unfamiliar room, yet to Finney it glowed with unearthly radiance, and there he met the
Saviour face to face. Such was the melting of his heart at this
sight that he wept like a child and bathed the sacred feet with
his tears. When the young man at last returned to the front
office, the great oak logs he had rolled into the fireplace were
reduced to a few glowing ashes! He would have estimated
that his absence had consumed only a few minutes, but now he
realized that it was deep into the night! He started to take a
seat by the dying embers, when lo, the Holy Spirit descended
upon him again in waves of love like the fanning of immense
wings. The very breath of God breathed its life into his soul.
He wept aloud, giving voice to the unutterable gushings of joy
and love that filled his being.

"Oh!" said he, "I shall die if these waves continue to pass over me. Lord, I cannot bear any more!" Yet in all this he had no fear of death.

At one time, the thought of leaving his beloved law profession to enter the ministry would have staggered Finney. But now, after receiving these baptisms of the Spirit, he was quite willing to preach the Gospel. Indeed he found that he was unwilling to do anything else! He wrote, "I had no disposition to make money. I had no hungering and thirsting after worldly pleasures and amusements in any direction. My whole mind was taken up with Jesus and His salvation; and the world seemed to me of very little consequence. Nothing . . . could be put in competition with the worth of souls; and no labor, I thought, could be so sweet, and no employment so exalted as that of holding up Christ to a dying world."

Young Finney began his ministry immediately by witnessing to everyone he saw in the village. Said he, "I cannot remember one with whom I spoke, who was not soon after converted." The slain of the Lord fell under the power of his testimony everywhere he went. His words stuck like arrows in the hearts of his listeners — prophetic of the power he was to exert through the Holy Ghost in all the golden years of his ensuing evangelistic endeavors.

Having had no regular training for the ministry, Finney neither expected nor desired to labor with cultivated congregations in large towns or cities. He made up his mind to go into new settlements and preach as best he could in schoolhouses, barns and groves. Accordingly, he turned his face toward Evans Mills, twenty-five miles northwest of Adams, and to Antwerp, sixteen or eighteen miles still farther north.

Stopping first at Utica to secure his missionary commission, he found himself inadvertantly captured by a new and delightful consideration — a fast growing fascination, bordering on love, for one Miss Lydia Andrews, whose Christian graces charmed him indeed. He was not long in deciding that this matter would bear more serious attention later.

Though not rugged in health, Finney never spared himself in striving to get the Gospel to his neglected people. Many hours each day were spent in calling from house to house. He attended prayer meetings. He preached night after night, and oftentimes afternoons. On his faithful steed, he sped from one town to another, and in ever-widening circles through forests to other communities.

What a mission field! In many places the inhabitants were entirely destitute of any religious services, and most of them had never before sung a hymn. At first, Finney's ardent discourses were received by his hearers with astonishment, then with anger, then finally, under the power of the Spirit, with great and almost unanimous prostration beneath the load of their sins, which resulted in their conversion.

At Antwerp, one of Finney's meetings was visited by an aged man living in a community three miles distant.

"Come and help us," urged the man, "for we have never had a service in our village."

"Tomorrow at five, then," agreed Finney, "tell everyone to come."

When the young preacher arrived the next day, the schoolhouse was so full he could find standing room only at the open door. He gave out a hymn, and while the people were attempting to sing it, he cried to God for the message that would make the deepest impression upon his hearers. The Spirit strongly impressed him to preach on the wickedness of Sodom. He had not been speaking long when he noticed angry looks take form on the faces of his congregation. He could not understand what he was saying that would offend them. However, it seemed that as he further proceeded with his narrative, their anger rose higher and higher. Then, unaccountably, an awful solemnity settled down upon them. They fell from their seats in every direction and cried for mercy. Wrote Finney later, "If I had had a sword in each hand, I could not have cut them off their seats as fast as they fell. Indeed nearly the whole congregation were either on their knees or prostrate . . .in less than two minutes. . . . Everyone prayed for himself, who was able to speak at all."

Since no one was now paying any attention to what he was saying, Finney stopped preaching. He surveyed the astonishing scene before him. There, in the middle of the house, sat the old man who had invited him there to preach. He was gazing around in utter consternation.

"Can't you pray?" shouted Finney in a voice raised almost to a scream to make him hear.

Down on his knees went the gentleman and began pouring out his soul to God in tones deep and stentorian. No one paid the least attention to him, whereupon Finney called out loudly to anyone who would lend him an ear, "You are not in hell yet; and now let me direct you to Christ."

He tried to encourage the people by holding forth the Gospel to them, but still scarcely any paid him heed. Finally he began dealing with individuals one by one. As soon as one seeker found Jesus, he set him to praying for someone else. It was a glorious sight. All night long the meeting lasted, and even into the next afternoon.

It was at this afternoon meeting that Finney ascertained the name of the community. Much to his surprise, it was "Sodom." The only pious man in the village had been nicknamed "Lot" by his fellow townsmen. And this was the individual who had invited Finney there to preach! No wonder the people had looked angry the day before! They supposed the minister had chosen his subject and preached to them in that manner because they were so wicked as to be called, "Sodom."

Said Finney, "This was a striking coincidence; but so far as I was concerned, it was altogether accidental." It could be attributed only to the Holy Spirit's leadership.

Many were the souls saved at this place, and far-reaching were the results — typical of the miraculous visitations of God in Finney's meetings throughout his evangelistic career.

From Evans Mills and Antwerp, Finney proceeded to other needy areas. During his meetings both in Rome, New York, and in Utica, it was commonly remarked that no one could be in the town or pass through it without being aware of the presence of God. Indeed, there were several cases of persons just stopping for a meal or to spend the night, being powerfully convicted and converted before leaving town.

Charles G. Finney's fame spread rapidly, and so great did the demand for his ministry become that he found it difficult to pull himself away long enough to claim the bonny Lydia for his bride. But this was not all. Even a greater difficulty lay before him. After the wedding he turned back to Evans Mills to obtain transportation for their goods to that place, intending to return for his bride the next week. This was in October, 1824. Before he could carry out his plans, winter had melted into spring, and spring had warmed into summer. In the meantime, he had been prevailed upon to hold evangelistic services, each one of several weeks' duration, in three needy communities — Perch River, Brownville and Le Rayville. This experience proved prophetic

of Finney's entire ministry. Personal plans, if he had any, were
subject to the overruling of the Holy Spirit and the call of the
needy.

Sparks from the young evangelist's meetings began to fly far
and wide. In fact, they kindled revival fires all over the eastern
part of the United States. One thrilling instance relates to the
awakening experienced among the lumbermen of northern
Pennsylvania. These men spent their winters getting out their
lumber, which, in the spring, was easily floated down the Delaware River to Philadelphia. On one of these trips to the big
city, a group of woodsmen attended Mr. Finney's meetings, and
several of them were genuinely converted. Back to the wilderness they went, testifying to their families and fellow-laborers,
and praying for the outpouring of the Holy Spirit there. God
immediately answered their cries. A revival broke out and
spread through the forests in great power and glory. Many
were convicted and converted who had not attended any meetings — people who were almost as ignorant as heathen.

One of these was Jack. His work had taken him far from
home this early spring of 1829. So, in the depth of the timber
he had put up a little shanty where he stayed all alone. A few
weeks before this he would have scoffed if anyone had suggested that he would be afraid. Afraid? He? Jack afraid?
Ridiculous!

But Jack was not long out on this trip until he felt strangely
that things were different than they had ever been before. The
loneliness was wearing on him! And he *was* afraid! It was not
the dangers of the woods that pinched his heart with terror
. . . but . . . the way he had been living! His sins! Let people
call him what they might, this was awful! Why, *no one* could
stand the sight of such sins for long. Just let them try it!

So reflected Jack in the increasingly eery silence round
about him, until the load of guilt became so heavy he broke
beneath it.

"It's true, God Almighty!" Jack wailed into the forest's vast-
ness. "It's all true!" He crumpled to his knees. "There's nothing
hid from You — and if there is, drag it out, and take it all from
off me!"

What waves of contrition and heart-opening reached the
throne of heaven that day, only Jack and the Saviour know,
but as the echoes of a lumberman's cry died away to stillness,

the Spirit of the living God bent low to earth and made a sinner's stained soul as white as snow.

Jack had never attended a prayer meeting, had never heard a prayer or a testimony in his life, but the transformation wrought in his soul that day was something to talk about! He hurried through underbrush and stumbled over fallen logs. A mile or two he floundered on, to break the good news to his friends. But lo! when he came upon them, they were not cutting lumber any more than he was cutting lumber. God had spoken to them, too, and they were having prayer!

Jack knelt in their midst. So happy was he that he laughed with holy joy, as with face upturned, by faith he beheld beyond the treetops his Saviour, whose blood had cleansed away his every sin.

"Thank You, Lord," he cried with rapture. "You got me down! You got me down! Yes, You got me down, and this is where I hope You'll keep me." He clapped his hands in sheer exultation. "And now, dear Lord," he continued, "since You've had so good luck with me, I hope You'll try other sinners, too!"

His prayer was answered! God marvelously set on fire that whole lumber region extending eighty miles in length. Five thousand people found the Lord, and all this without the help or preaching of the ministry, in an area so underprivileged that one of the young men testified he did not know his alphabet, and that in all his twenty years he had never attended a religious meeting.

Nor was the revival flame visible only on the land, for the Spirit of God moved upon the face of the water, and a multitude of seamen saw the great light. It was as if a shimmering aureole of heavenly blessing hovered over both land and sea. As ships drew near the American ports, and came within the zone of heavenly influence, sudden conviction and conversion settled down upon passengers and sailors alike. In one instance, the captain and his entire crew of thirty men found Christ out at sea, and entered the harbor rejoicing. The holy fire spread rapidly from ship to ship, and as each in time left the harbor of New York for foreign seas, the gospel flames were fanned to the ends of the earth.

Thus Finney was used to win to the Lord not only thousands who sat under the sound of his voice, but he became the instrument in God's hands of precipitating a panoramic deluge of salvation upon vast multitudes who never saw him or heard him preach.

Finney's labors centered chiefly in the eastern states. However, they were not confined entirely to this area. He made two trips to England, where his Gospel messages were graciously blessed of the Lord. Neither was his ministry confined to the field of preaching, for Finney spent parts of many profitable years acting as president of Oberlin College, and as head of its Department of Theology. He also exerted a wide influence through his "Revival Lectures," which were published first in the *New York Evangelist,* and later in book form. Notwithstanding, it can be said that unquestionably his greatest fruitage sprang from his evangelistic endeavors, which embraced not only the preaching of the Word, but his personal work, private interviews, and, most important of all, his life of prayer. For Finney himself was an ardent, tireless intercessor, who incited others everywhere he went, to pray. Among his noble army of faithful prayer warriors, the names of Father Nash and Abel Clary will be remembered as long as prayer history is made and read.

At the height of the great awakening in the winter of 1857 and 1858, noonday prayer meetings were in progress in New York, Philadelphia, Chicago, and many other cities, with as high as two and three thousand in attendance at a single service.

During one of Mr. Finney's meetings in Boston, a man testified that on his journey east from Omaha, Nebraska, he had found a continuous prayer meeting all the way. Said he, "We call it two thousand miles from Omaha to Boston; and here was a prayer meeting about two thousand miles in extent."

It was estimated that for a period of almost two months at this time, fifty thousand persons were converted weekly throughout the country, the number spiraling to a total of no less than five hundred thousand conversions within the year.

Thus did Charles G. Finney sweep across our land like a glorious gale from heaven, heralding the message of salvation to unnumbered throngs. Such as this was the conflagration set on fire by the youth who overcame the fear of man in a nameless woodland north of Adams, New York, one October day in 1821 — the youth who abandoned himself unconditionally to the disposal of the Almighty.

Prisoner of the Lord

THE SHARP TOOTH of a stiff wind swept over angry seas and bit cruelly into the northeastern coast of England that long ago March of 1666. It sent children scurrying into warm, snug houses in the little town at the water's edge, and shrieked eerily through holes and caves scooped out of solid rock – the solid rock of a frowning cliff overlooking the troubled waters that stretched as far as eye could see. Upon the cliff towered Scarborough Castle, a grand and mighty fortress, through which George Fox, weak and ill had been dragged only a few days before to a hole all his own in the windswept crag.

Much of George's last few years had been spent in prison. In fact, he had come here straight from several months' confinement in Lancaster jail where he had languished because he had refused to "swear" in court, and because he had spoken so staunchly against the unjust administration of the officers.

His first night in these new quarters beneath the castle had been a sleepless one. One whole side of the cave was open to the sea, and a storm had blown the rain in so sharply that all he had was drenched. When he had managed to build a fire by which to warm himself and to dry out his abode, the smoke had billowed up so thick he had scarcely been able to find his way about or to get his breath. Things could not continue thus, he decided. So he laid out fifty shillings of his own money to screen himself against the elements and to make a sort of chimney for the smoke. But no sooner had he settled down in more tolerable circumstances than he was removed into a worse niche, which afforded neither chimney nor fire hearth.

What should he do? The merciless tempest was driving rain and snow wildly into every cranny of his bleak cell. The last thread of his clothes, bed blanket, and mattress was drenched to the dripping point. Little rivers wound in and out the rough floor stones, settling into pools and miniature lakes, so that the

prisoner had need to take care where he stepped, to say nothing
of the hopelessness of finding a dry spot upon which to sit
or lie down.

George stood surveying his predicament. He pulled his
sodden cloak closer about his shivering form, then stooped to
pick up a bit of broken earthenware.

He skimmed water out of a pool and threw it over the cliff

"This platter won't hold much," he observed to himself, "but
if the storm should hold off a little, I might be able to rid myself of some of the wetness underfoot . . ." He skimmed water
out of a pool and threw it over the cliff. ". . . and I may be able
to find a bed on the floor if not on my mattress," he finished
heroically.

But when George and the platter had done their best, the
unfortunate exile, having no fire by which to dry his clothes,
languished in misery, his body benumbed with cold, his fingers
swollen to twice their natural size.

"I am as a man buried alive," he mused contemplatively.

And so he was. Friends often essayed to visit him with
gifts of dry clothing and needful comforts, but seldom were
they permitted to see him. Finally, he was obliged to hire a
woman of the castle to bring him food and water, else he would
have starved. Even then the soldiers often grabbed the provisions
out of her hands before she could deliver them to George. Thus,
he was commonly limited to only a threepenny loaf every three
weeks, and water in which wormwood had been steeped.

In all this, however, the intrepid man of God kept the fires
of faith and victory burning in his heart. His solitary confine-

ment gave him leisure to commune at length with the Almighty, from whence came new and supernatural boldness to wage warfare to the finish against sin and worldliness. It gave him time, when his fingers were not too stiff, to write letters of encouragement and comfort, warning and advice, to his fellow comrades in suffering. For George Fox was looked up to now by thousands of people as their leader in spite of the fact that he had never intended to found a new sect or organize a religious body of workers.

It had all started when he was but a child — a very "unchildlike" child, it might be said. From his earliest years he obeyed religiously his tender conscience, and sought after God. One day, sorely vexed with the lack of spirituality around him, he thought the Lord Himself drew near.

"Thou seest how young people go together into vanity," the Saviour said, "and old people into the earth; therefore thou must forsake all, both old and young, and be a stranger unto them."

This command, which George felt to be a divine one, he set about following at once. At the age of nineteen, he broke off all friendship with his acquaintances, took leave of his relatives, and, that he might truly live a separate and retired life, left his father's house in Drayton, Leicestershire, England, on September 9, 1643, to become a pilgrim and a wanderer in the earth.

He was found in cities, tiny villages, sleeping under hedges, studying his Bible in a hollow tree, and in every imaginable as well as unimaginable place. So ruinous was this mode of life to ordinary clothing that George ordered made for himself that famous pair of leathern breeches which have since become historical.

Many wonderful things were revealed to the young man as he sought heavenly guidance, wisdom and heart purity. One was that God did not dwell in houses and temples made with hands, but in people's hearts. For this conviction and for calling buildings for worship, "steeple-houses" or "meeting houses," instead of "churches," he was to suffer much persecution, as well as for refusing to go to war to destroy men's never-dying souls for whom Christ gave His life. He saw Christ as a refiner's fire that could consume the old self life, the unsanctified will, and all that could not yield itself to the death of the cross. With this revelation, George Fox was forever set at liberty. In that hour, too, there came to him that consciousness of the "inner light" —

the divine light in the regenerated heart which if followed honestly and truly, he felt would lead to God, and that without the aid of any human ordinances. This "light," or the leading of the Holy Spirit, he ever sought to follow, cost what it would.

Immediately he went to Manchester to visit some professing Christians, and declare to them what he believed to be the true doctrine. His words were few and halting, but they were nevertheless piercing, as some found to their eternal good. This was the beginning of George Fox's ministry. Some of his hearers were convinced of the truth, and accepted as their rule the inward divine teaching of the Lord. But, as might be expected, there were many others who could not endure this preaching that searched to the marrow of the soul — this call to holiness of heart and life.

In about 1649, his followers and converts began to assemble together, and sat in silence to wait upon God until, as His Spirit led one and another to give witness in prayer or speech or song, they obeyed. At one time when George had made many converts in Yorkshire, and his fame had spread, he went to a village to speak in a great public outdoor meeting. The people poured in from all quarters to hear him. George mounted a haystack. The people settled themselves to listen. But no words came from the preacher's lips! For several hours they waited! They naturally began to grow impatient, but an old clergyman stepped forward.

"Peace, friends," he quieted them, "people in olden days often waited as long as this to hear our Saviour speak."

At last, George felt himself permitted of God to open his mouth in utterance, and his burning words, poured forth from a Spirit-anointed heart, did a mighty work in the souls of many present that day.

When questioned later as to his strange behavior, his answer was characteristic. "I was commanded," he explained, "to famish them for words," so dependent had they always been on the instrumentality of man.

Not only were the utterances of this man penetrating and fearful, but so was his whole aspect. Tall and of dignified bearing, he walked among men with the air of one living in another world, yet clothed in kindliness withal. His eyes especially seemed to attract the attention of those to whom he spoke.

Once when those eyes fell upon a man who was arguing for

the wrong, he cried out in terror, "Do not pierce me so with thine eyes! Keep thine eyes off me!"

At another time a hostile crowd suddenly stopped their clamor and cried out with one accord, "Look at his eyes! Look at his eyes!"

And yet again when he was riding through an angry mob in a city where men were ready to take his life, they dared not touch him, "Oh, Oh!" they cried, "See, he shines! He glisters!"

"I was exercised," wrote George in his journal near the beginning of his ministry, in his quaint, matter-of-fact style, "in going to courts to cry for justice and in speaking to judges and justices to do justly; in warning such as kept public houses, in testifying against wakes, feasts, May games, and sports, plays and shows, which trained up people to vanity and looseness, and taught them to forget God. In fairs also, and in markets, I was made to declare against their deceitful merchandise and cheating, warning all to deal justly, to speak truth, and let their yea be yea, and their nay be nay, and to do unto others as they would have others do unto them, warning them of that great and terrible day of the Lord that would come to all. I was moved also to cry against the montebanks playing off their tricks on the stage, for they stirred the people's mind to vanity. I was much exercised toward the schoolmasters and schoolmistresses, warning them to teach the children sobriety in the fear of the Lord. I was made to warn fathers and mothers to take care that their children and servants might be trained up in the fear of the Lord, and that they themselves should be therein examples and patterns of sobriety and virtue to them."

Never in the whole course of his life could George see anything sinful, or oppressive, or a sham, without a burning desire to remedy it, and so he always went at it full tilt, heedless of what might be involved to himself in pain and suffering and persecution.

No wonder the court officers of the land hated him and ridiculed his preaching.

"All men should tremble at the word of the Lord," George declared in his preaching one day at court.

A sneer hissed around the room, "Quakers and Tremblers is the name for such people," declared Justice Bennett scornfully.

And so George Fox and his followers, whom some had named "children of light," were first called "Quakers" by a man who might have been surprised if he could have known that centuries after, thousands of people all over the world would still feel honored to be called by the title he had given in a moment of mockery.

Having stirred up such hatred against himself among the justices of the land, the natural consequence was that George often found himself in jail! His first imprisonment resulted from his standing to his feet in the middle of a church service, and differing with what the clergyman was preaching, after which he proclaimed to the people the salvation of Jesus Christ.

"As I spoke among them," George related to his friends, "the officers came, took me away, and put me in a nasty, stinking prison; the smell whereof got into my nose, that it very much annoyed me!"

Poor George! The time soon came when he forgot to be particular as to the atmosphere of his prisons, so accustomed did he become to them.

Once a lady visiting the dungeons of Colchester Castle approached the custodian, "Is this where George Fox was imprisoned?" she asked curiously.

"There is no record of it," replied the man, "but it is very likely. Fox saw the inside of most of the prisons of England!"

The man spoke truly, and what prisons they were! Usually underground, unless of the cliff type in which George later found himself beneath Scarborough Castle, they were filthy and abominable in the extreme. The common sewer of the town ran through some, so that the air was full of vile, noxious gases. In York Castle alone, five Quakers died for no other reason than because of the impure air. Frogs and toads, newts and all sorts of vermin had their abiding place there. A stone seat generally ran around the room, which was always wet and always cold. The sunshine never penetrated these drear abodes. Yet, never was it known that the heart or flesh of George Fox failed him when, again and again, he was "brought up short against a prison wall." In fact, he turned his adversity into blessing to others and frequently saw the conversion of his own jailors! Besides, like Paul, he considered himself a prisoner, not of men, but of the Lord, and was content.

George's followers were equally as courageous. As his teachings spread, so also did the persecutions, and it is said that at one time there were two thousand men and women Quakers in jail in England for conscience' sake. As their leader was more than once dragged for miles on end, beaten and stoned, despoiled of his goods, so were they. In London, on one Sunday alone, some eighty Quakers were beaten, had their coats and clothes torn off their backs, and then were driven outside the city and thrown into ditches and ponds. Even children were not exempt. Eleven boys and four girls were sent to prison in Bristol. Others were flogged by the police till they became a mass of bruises. A sixteen-year-old girl died in prison for her faith. All this, chiefly for not paying tithes to the corrupt clergy of the day, for not attending recognized churches, for refusing to take the oath, and for failing to take off their hats in homage to another.

Little by little, however, favorable sentiment concerning the Quakers sprang up, at least in people's hearts, if not openly. At one time, five men and women Quakers were ordered to be conveyed to Leicester jail because they planned to hold a meeting in a private home, (probably that of Judge Fell), instead of in a church. But no one seemed willing to haul them to prison.

"We are busy with harvest," the country folk said.

"Yes," joined in others, "let them take their arrest warrant and convey themselves."

A Quaker's word was as good as his bond any day, and well the people knew it! As the sentenced group drove through town in their own wagons, some with their open Bibles, and one woman with her spinning-wheel in her lap, onlookers were "mightily affected."

The suffering of these, his comrades, moved George as nothing else would. As far as he was concerned, he could suffer gladly. But to see his "children" — particularly the women and little ones — tortured and persecuted was almost more than he could bear.

For their sakes he spared neither trouble nor pains. He boldly forced his way into the houses of those high in office and even into the presence of Cromwell himself.

At one time when George was ready to take his leave, Cromwell caught him by the hand, saying with tears in his eyes, "Come again to my house, for if thou and I were but an hour a day together, we should be nearer to one another. I wish you no more harm than I do to my own soul."

As George was departing he was brought into a large hall where the gentlemen of the palace dined.

"What is this for?" George demanded.

"It is Cromwell's wish, sir, that you should dine with them."

This was considered a great honor indeed, but George replied, "Tell the protector I will neither eat of his bread nor drink of his drink."

When this plain message was given to Cromwell, he remarked, "Now I see that there is a people risen up that I cannot win either with gifts, honors, offices, or places, but all other sects and people I can."

It was not only in England that Quakerism's light shone, for, as George in 1661 wrote in his journal, "Several friends were moved to go beyond the seas to publish truth in foreign countries." In 1669, soon after he had seen his wife, Margaret, former widow of Judge Fell, released from prison, George himself journeyed to the West Indies and America, particularly Maryland and New England. He had previously ministered as far afield as Scotland, Ireland, Holland and Germany. George suffered a great deal during these voyages. It began to be plain now to all who knew him that his health had become seriously undermined during his last long imprisonment on the cliff. Indeed, though they did not know it then, it was thoroughly broken down and never rallied fully again.

Everywhere George went in the New World, he urged that slaves should be set free as soon as proper employment could be found for them. It was here too that he felt led, because of some wide-spreading scandals against the Quakers, to draw up a formal confession of the Quaker faith.

He spent two years traveling about in Maryland and New England, employing his days in tedious journeyings through woods and bogs, and across rivers over which he was forced to make his horses swim. Some of his meetings lasted four or five days, and were attended by people who must have traveled at least a week to get there. His missionary journey as a whole was a successful one, and those "convinced of the truth" whom he left in his wake were sufficient reward for the most toilsome of wanderings.

While Puritans as a general rule looked upon the North American Indian as their natural enemy, there were no people in whom George took more interest than these. He impressed upon his followers their duties to the red man with such good effect that as late as 1812 a historian tells us that "the best defence against the Indians" in those days "was the dress of a Quaker."

At last George felt his "mind free of America" and embarked on a perilous voyage to his loved ones across the sea, only to fall into jail almost immediately upon his arrival. He employed himself while thus laid aside in writing tracts and epistles. Always he begged his followers to show themselves an example of unworldliness, especially in dress.

The year 1690 saw George Fox triumphantly borne into the Kingdom above, "as a vessel, full-freighted rides into harbor on the calm bosom of a spring tide." One of his last utterances was, "Now I am clear — fully clear." He had fulfilled the calling for which God intended him to live.

No longer did it matter that he had suffered eight different imprisonments during his lifetime, from dungeons below the streets to holes in the storm-scoured cliff 'neath Scarborough Castle. Earth's shackles at last had loosed their grip and he was free forevermore.

Carlyle says, "No grander thing was ever done than when George Fox, stitching himself into a suit of leather, went forth determined to find truth for himself, and to do battle for it against all superstition, bigotry, and intolerance."

"Above All Selfish Views"

MORE THAN TWO HUNDRED years ago, a lonely horseback rider dismounted in the depth of one of New York State's wildest forests, and dropped instantly to his knees. What he had seen through the thick branches that overhung the path ahead might have looked comparatively harmless to an unknowing traveler. But the lazy spirals of smoke curling upward into the calm blue of this early summer day in 1774, told David Brainerd that wigwams squatted not far distant — the wigwams of Indians, who, he had been informed, were the most savage of all the tribes in the wilderness at this time. Their very fierceness had challenged the young missionary to reach them with the Gospel of Jesus Christ. And now here he was, at the threshold of their camp.

The youth, always depreciative of his own ability, knelt long in the woods, imploring the succor of the Almighty and pleading for a new baptism of divine love for the souls of this people, so unlovely, so wretched. His fervor mounted high above his caution, until his supplications were no longer confined to the silent heaving of the breast and the breathing forth of wordless prayer, but were voiced in passionate pleadings, and in cries so ardent that they reached the ears of the ever wary camp, only a few hundred yards away.

In a matter of seconds, the stealthy footsteps of a dozen braves intruded upon Brainerd's sanctum under the trees; sharp, wicked eyes fixed their gaze upon his upturned face; sly, deft fingers silently fitted a dozen arrows to a dozen bows. The forest held its breath.

Then, as one man, the whole fierce company stood transfixed.

Expressionless as they had steeled themselves to be, their savage visages, unguarded now, turned to utter wonder and amazement. One brave went so far as to point toward the kneeling man, but his pointing was as needless as it was unheeded, for every eye had seen. Now it slithered closer to the stranger — the object of their gaze — a rattler, huge and venomous. At the very feet of the paleface it coiled, drew its head back angrily, flicked its forked tongue satanically. In a moment the reptile would strike the intruder. No need then for Indians' bows and arrows!

At the very feet of the paleface it coiled

The red men waited, breathless, charmed.

But when the deadly reptile should have sunk its fangs into the hapless supplicant, a strange thing happened, never before heard of in woodland lore or Indian tradition. The serpent loosed its coils, hushed its hissing, and glided away, as harmless as the breezes in the treetops. There was a moment of awesome wonder. Then the warriors looked at one another in mutual understanding, and filed back to their supper fires as noiselessly as they had come.

David Brainerd prayed on until the shades of evening closed about him, then lay down on nature's bed and went to sleep.

The following morning, he set out for the Indian camp of his quest. Whether hostility awaited him, or even death, he knew not. But his heart was fixed to suffer any sacrifice for the souls of these Indians without a preacher. What was his surprise, then, when upon approaching their midst, he was greeted with almost reverential courtesy. They extended their hands in friendship, and offered him food and hospitality. In answer to his inquiry as to the meaning of such a welcome, he was told the thrilling story of the rattler's strange behavior the evening before.

"The Great Spirit is with the paleface!" they all affirmed with much solemnity. "The Great Spirit is with the paleface!"

Though David Brainerd was profoundly thankful for this evidence of the providential care of God, he rejoiced more because the incident, fearful though its outcome could have been, had opened a door effectual among the Indians, whereby he was able to do much good.

Not so spectacular, however, had been his attempts to reach other tribes. Neither in the future was his way to the heathen to be so miraculously opened up. Always in poor health, David Brainerd suffered untold deprivations in his many travels among the widely scattered Indian tribes of his special care.

In ministering to those at Kaunameek, New York, then at the forks of the Delaware and later on the banks of the Susquehannah, he trekked thousands of miles, all on foot or by horseback, wallowing through swamps, toiling over rocky foothills, pushing his way through dense forests and over bleak, windswept mountains, traversing desolate wasteland, and picking his way up trackless gorges. He frequently spent his nights lying out in the open woods, and during one journey alone, to his Indians on the Susquehannah, he lodged on the ground for several weeks at a time.

On this journey Brainerd, his interpreter and two Indians found by far the most difficult and dangerous traveling they had ever seen. "We had scarcely anything else but lofty mountains, deep valleys and hideous rocks to make our way through," wrote Brainerd in his diary. "Near night, my beast that I rode upon, hung (caught) one of her legs in the rocks, and fell down under me; but through divine goodness, I was not hurt. However, she broke her leg; and being in such a hideous place, and near thirty miles from any house, I saw nothing that could be done to preserve her life, and so was obliged to kill her, and to prosecute my journey on foot . . . Just at dark, we kindled a fire, cut up a few branches, and made a shelter over our heads, to save us from the frost, which was very hard that night. Committing ourselves to God by prayer, we lay down on the ground and slept quietly."

On another journey, traveling from Rockciticus, New Jersey, to the Delaware River, Brainerd lost his way in the wilderness. Nightfall descended early upon him, for the November day had been unusually bleak and overcast. He wandered over rocks and mountains, down "hideous steeps," through swamps, and "most dreadful and dangerous places." Few stars penetrated the inky sky, making every step an advance into the unknown. To add to his extremity, Brainerd himself was much debilitated at the time, suffering an excruciating headache, accompanied by nausea. On he groped, pinched with cold, and for several hours despaired of any better prospect than that of lying out in the woods all night. However, through the goodness of God he came upon a cabin where he received kindly entertainment.

On a subsequent journey to Susquehannah with his interpreter he was less fortunate, however. After enduring great hardships and "fatigues" on their way through a rugged wilderness, having lodged one night in the open woods, they were overtaken one evening by a northeasterly storm so tempestuous that they feared they must perish. Having no manner of shelter, and not being able to make a fire in so great a rain, they could see no advantage in stopping. So on they went, in the scant hope of finding a refuge, without which, indeed, it seemed impossible to live the night through.

To add to their dire extremity, their horses fell sick, having eaten poison at the place of their lodging the night before in the absence of proper provender. Now they could neither be ridden nor led, but must be driven by Brainerd and his companion as they stumbled along on foot.

Again, a merciful God looked down in pity upon his helpless servants and guided their way to a bark hut where they spent the night.

Under conditions such as these, David Brainerd pushed on. As an arrow winging to its mark, so Brainerd sped to fulfill his divine calling. In a single day he traveled one hundred miles, and from March to November, 1745, he rode more than three thousand miles.

For lack of better accommodations, Brainerd once lived in a wigwam with the Indians. During this time, he conducted his services in the dwelling of the chief. Heavy volumes of smoke arose from the huge camp fire, wrapping the preacher and his audience in such dense clouds that they could not see him, nor he them. Gusts of wind blew the ashes and dust from the fire into his eyes and mouth until he was nearly choked. Severe headaches ensued after these services, but David Brainerd remained many long months, although for days on end, when the heavy rains fell, he was unable to move out of the wigwam.

At one place in his travels, the young missionary found the Indians preparing for a sacrifice and dance. So absorbed were they that he sought in vain to gather them together for a meeting. Not willing to concede defeat, he tarried all night with them, walking to and fro in prayer, as the idolatrous reveling increased in crescendo and gruesomeness. When the savages finally ate the flesh of the sacrifice and retired to their wigwams, Brainerd, being entirely alone on the island as to any Christian company, his mind and heart much pained and oppressed, crept into a little crib made for corn, and slept on the poles, hoping that on the morrow he might yet "find opportunity to get the blessed gospel to these wretched souls."

Indeed, anything was made to pass for a resting place, as this tireless hero of the cross sought out the benighted red men. A buffalo skin came to be a luxury, while a pallet of straw or a few green branches served the purpose on most occasions.

Even when he was privileged to enjoy the comfort of a little cabin in the woods built with his own hands, his deep concern for the conversion of the Indians burdened him by day and robbed him of his sleep at night. Often when evening came he was so depressed by the idea that he had failed to do what God expected and what his eager spirit was keen to render, and was so absorbed in confession and supplication that he forgot to take his simple supper and to provide himself with either a fire or a comfortable bed.

No wonder, then, that Brainerd's health, precarious enough at the beginning of his missionary endeavors, grew steadily more feeble. His diary often recorded fits of fever, coughing of blood, cold sweats, pains in his head, chest and back, nausea, weakness, weariness and melancholy. He rode many a mile when he was scarcely able to sit on his horse. Yet in all this, his indomitable spirit would not succumb to inactivity or an easier way of service for the Master.

On one occasion of extreme debility he wrote, ". . . was able to do very little except discourse a while of divine things to my . . . people." Then because he felt his spirit should have been more ardent and his message more fruitful, he added, "Was scarcely ever more shamed and confounded in myself than now. I was sensible that there were numbers of God's people who knew I was then out upon a design (or at least the pretense) of doing something for God, and in His cause, among the poor Indians and they were ready to suppose that I was 'fervent in spirit.' But oh, the heartless frame of mind that I felt, filled me with confusion! Oh (methought) if God's people knew me, as God knows, they would not think so highly of my zeal and resolution for God, as perhaps now they do! I could not but desire they should see how heartless and irresolute I was, that they might be undeceived and 'not think of me above what they ought to think.' "

In spite of David Brainerd's deprecatory estimate of himself and his endeavors, however, God thought it meet to honor his humble servant with some precious fruits for his labors. After a whole year of seeming failure, the truth began to take hold. In one assembly a divine influence manifestly accompanied the preaching of the Word, and several "stupid creatures" who were scarcely ever moved with any concern, now were shocked and roused at heart so that many tears and sobs were to be seen and heard among them. A lively eagerness and intenseness of mind appeared and they seemed to watch and wait for the dropping of God's Word, as the thirsty earth for the "former and latter rain."

At the same time, numbers of men and women, old and young, bore the aspect of condemned malefactors bound toward the place of execution, with a heavy solicitude clouding their faces, "a lively emblem," said Brainerd, "of the solemn day of accounts, a mixture of heaven and hell, of joy and anguish inexpressible."

When numbers of his poor Indians had at last been converted, among them an eighty-year-old woman so ignorant, feeble and childish that it seemed impossible that she could grasp the simplest truths, Brainerd remarked, "I was ready to think then that I should never again despair of the conversion of any man or woman living, be they who or what they would."

Another woman was brought to such an "agony in seeking Christ that the sweat ran off her face for a considerable time, although the evening was very cold, and her bitter cries indicated in a most affecting way the inward anguish of her heart."

One Sabbath day, a man, a weary, heavy-laden soul, after having suffered long the buffetings of the Evil One, found safe anchorage for eternity in the blessed Rock of Ages. "I saw with my heart something unspeakably good and lovely — something I had never seen before," he told Brainerd later. "It stole away my heart whether I would or no. I did not give my heart away as I had intended and tried to do, but it went away of itself after that glory — the glory I found in Christ my Lord."

Nothing heartened Brainerd so much as to see his poor Indians, who a day before had been hallooing and yelling in their idolatrous feasts and drunken frolics, now plead with God in life and death earnestness for a part in His salvation. "Guttum-mauhalummeh! Guttummauhalummeh!" they cried. "Have mercy upon me! Have mercy upon me!"

At the close of one short year spent preaching to the Indians at Crossweegsung in New Jersey, Brainerd wrote in his journal, "What amazing things has God wrought in this space of time, for this poor people! What a surprising change appears in their tempers and behavior! How are morose and savage pagans, in this short period, transferred into agreeable, affectionate and humble Christians! And their drunken and pagan howlings turned into devout and fervent praises to God; they who were sometimes in darkness are now become light in the Lord."

Once he preached through a drunken interpreter, a man so intoxicated that he could hardly stand up. Yet scores were converted through that sermon — results indicative of the tremendous power of God in answering the prayers of His true servant.

Consumed with a fiery passion to see the heathen saved, Brainerd feared nothing so much as to outlive his usefulness, and when the last moment of his earthly life had nearly come, he said sublimely, "I declare, now I am dying, I would not have spent my life otherwise for the whole world." Wasted with consumption, he died at the age of twenty-nine.

William Carey read Brainerd's life and he was so moved by it that he went to India. Henry Martyn read his life, and by its impulse he went to India. Payson read it as a young man of twenty years, and said he had never in all his life been so impressed. Robert Murray McCheyne read it, and was powerfully moved by it to prayer.

Though Brainerd spent only three short years in active Christian service, so far was he "above all selfish views," and so extensive, so effective had been his holy influence that Wesley exhorted his followers, "Let every preacher read carefully over the 'Life of David Brainerd.' Let us be followers of him, as he was in Christ, in absolute self-devotion, in total deadness to the world, and in fervent love to God and man. Let us but secure this point and the world will fall under our feet."

Trail of Eternal Glory

"No MONEY YET?" Joey accosted her husband as he shut the kitchen door behind him.

Billy had come in from the mines singing and praising the Lord as usual. He had always assured Joey that the Lord would provide their needs. Now her greeting struck him as a sly reproof for his "empty-headed" faith, as Joey might have termed it.

For a moment Billy's countenance fell. He cared not for the personal thrust, if such it was, but he could not have his Lord's Word discredited.

"N — no." He hesitated, then went on, "'Tis strange, isn't it, I've worked a whole month and no wages yet?" Then brightening, "But the Lord'll see us through. Just wait and see."

"But there's no bread in the house," Joey persisted, "and the children are cryin' for it."

"No bread?" Billy softened. He had not known their need was quite so desperate.

"No bread," Joey emphasized. Then she straightened, as one taking command of a situation. "Billy," she induced him, "go up to the Captain and ask him to lend you a few shillings. He is well able and we are so poor."

Billy wasn't the kind to borrow, such a practice being as it was, not only against his better judgment, but, more pertinently, contrary to his trust in the Lord to supply his needs. However, he would do it just this once for Joey's sake and the children's. So off he went to the Captain, who let him have ten shillings.

Homeward Billy hurried, whistling and praising the Lord for the Captain's kindness, when presently he came to the cottage of a friend and felt constrained to stop a minute. Here he found the family so poverty-stricken that he forgot his own distress. For though he had no bread at home, he did indeed have a few wrinkled potatoes and a slab of bacon. These people had nothing.

100

"Here," Billy offered with an irresistible impulse of pity, "Here, take these." And he threw five shillings down upon the bare table of his friend.

Along the road toward home went Billy, richer in heart if not in hand. He *would* like to stop at one more cottage, he thought. Perhaps Joey would not become too impatient if he took a moment to call upon this acquaintance. He would not stay long.

The door opened hospitably to Billy's knock and he entered. But such destitution greeted him, he could hardly hide his dismay. Why, there wasn't even a fire! The children were ragged and hungry, cold and sobbing. This was worse than what he had seen a few minutes before. What should he do? Could he give these people less than he had given the others? Into the hand of this friend Billy pressed his last five shillings.

He knew what Joey would say, but chiding or no chiding, he could do no differently.

"Well, William, have you seen the Captain?" were Joey's first words as Billy returned home.

"Yes," answered Billy cheerfully.

"Did he give you any money?"

"Yes, he was very kind. He gave me ten shillings."

"Where is it? Did you get any bread?"

"Why, no," Billy confessed, "You see I found two cottages so much worse off than we, that I gave it all away."

"Why, Billy Bray!" exclaimed Joey without any pretense of hiding her consternation. "Never in my life have I seen a fellow like you! You're enough to try the patience of anyone!"

"Now, now, Joey," Billy quieted her, "the good Lord won't be indebted to me for long. Just wait and see."

The next two or three days proved to be a fiery trial for Joey. In fact, her spirits were "mighty down," her outlook anything but sunny.

Then one evening she met Billy at the door with smiles illuminating all her face.

Something's up, thought Billy. *Wonder what the Lord's done now?*

"Our neighbor came to chat today," Joey tried to break her bit of news without too much display of excitement.

"Oh," Billy replied. "What then?"

"And she gave me a sovereign!" Joey burst out, unable to contain her ecstasy any longer.

"Praise the Lord!" shouted Billy, "There I said the Lord would not keep Himself in debt to me long. There's the ten shillings I borrowed and gave away, and ten shillings interest! Praise the Lord!"

In spite of frequent episodes such as this, Joey never altogether became accustomed to the surprising eccentricities of her unpredictable husband. One morning soon after this, Billy returned home from a walk, with two little children in his arms — a boy and a girl.

"Why, Billy," said Joey, "whose are these, and why did you bring them here?"

"Oh, Joey," Billy explained almost in tears, "the mother's dead, and the father's run away and left them playing by the stream, and so I brought them home to rear them up with ours."

"But we have four already," exclaimed Joey, throwing up her hands in desperation. "We can hardly provide for our own, to say nothing of two more. These will have to go to the workhouse, Billy."

"God can just as well feed them here as He can there," Billy avowed with finality. And he set the two little ones down on the floor to play with his own. "Here, my dears," he said tenderly, "this is your home now."

An evangelist who was stopping at Billy's house at the time was so touched with his host's big-heartedness in the face of so small an income, that he gave Billy five shillings on the spot. "Perhaps this will help to buy them food," he remarked, "and relieve your wife's distress."

"There, Joey," Billy shouted with joy, "the Lord has sent five shillings already, even before the children have eaten a penny loaf!"

Billy's exuberance was so great and the need so pressing that the evangelist could not feel easy until he had emptied his pockets of all the money he had — nearly three pounds altogether. Billy's gratitude knew no bounds, and in the prayer of thanksgiving which followed, such a blessing from heaven was showered upon them as would beggar description. As it turned out, Billy and Joey kept the homeless children until they were old enough to make their own living in the world.

Billy Bray's faith in the Lord and devotion to His cause was expressed not only in little deeds of kindness, but in larger exploits for the Kingdom. In his neighborhood there were many dark-minded, wicked people, and chapels were few. Billy felt that the Lord would have him build a chapel at Cross Lanes near his home. His mother gave him a small plot of ground. Accordingly, he began to clear the field, take away the hedge, and dig out the foundation for a house of worship to the Lord. Though he had many adversaries in executing his project, Billy proceeded, nothing doubting, and preached the first sermon at the site of the chapel while standing on the foundation stone.

"If this new chapel stands one hundred years," declared Billy, "and one soul be converted in it every year, that will be a hundred souls, and one soul is worth more than all Cornwall."

Billy was so happy with the prospect of future victories that he danced on the stone, and shouted, "Glory, glory, bless the Lord!"

A neighbor passed by and looked with disgust on Billy's high spirits and lofty aspirations.

"Give anything toward Billy Bray's chapel?" he repeated when approached for an offering. "Not I!"

When one of this man's horses became lame in the field and he lost many days' work at the mine, people said it was because the owner would not give anything to Billy Bray's chapel.

"But," said Billy, "the people should have remembered it was not my chapel, but the dear Lord's. It may be the Lord punished him for not giving anything to *His* chapel. I do not know."

As it happened, the chapel never proved to be much good to the man, for he died soon after. But Billy was enabled to build the chapel anyway, without his help, and for this he gratefully praised the Lord.

Many times in the process, in answer to Billy's prayers of faith, funds were miraculously provided just in time for the need. Near the completion of the building, Billy had enough timber for all the roof except one truss. He asked his Heavenly Father for some timber or enough money to buy some.

That same morning a preacher at some distance was on his knees praying when the Lord said to him, "Go down and give Billy Bray a pound note."

After breakfast the preacher made his way to Billy where he was working on the chapel and said, "What do you want a pound note for?"

"Why," replied Billy, "to buy timber to put a truss on that end of the chapel."

"Well, I never felt such a thing in all my life before," declared the preacher, "for while I was home praying this morning, it was always coming into my mind to go down and give you a pound note, and here it is."

Billy praised the Lord and got the timber he needed.

At another time when Billy had been given money for timber, he found that he had no way to haul it home to the Lord's house.

"I have a horse and cart," a neighbor reflected, "but my horse is stubborn. Can't get her to pull a thing."

"Would you let me try her?" Billy asked. "I need a way of conveyance so sorely."

"Try her if you want to," rejoined the man, "but she won't do you any good. I warn you."

Billy took the horse, hitched her to the cart and brought the timber home. It was all just as easy as that!

When Billy took the horse back he told the owner about her. "Never saw a better mare," he praised her. "Why, I didn't have to use the whip once, not even up the steepest hill."

"I didn't have to use the whip once," Billy said.

The neighbor listened in sheer astonishment. "You don't say," he finally ejaculated. "You must be an expert with horses. Why, I never saw such a thing! She won't pull for anyone else."

"The horse was not working for Billy Bray today," Billy explained in his own humble way. "If she had been, she would have been as mean as with anyone else. No, she was working this time for a very strong Company: Father, Son, and Holy

Ghost, whom horses, as well as angels, men and devils must obey. Yes, the Lord is an expert with horses!"

Some time later, Billy went around soliciting money toward covering the chapel roof with sheaves of reed. He collected only two pounds. To add to his concern, his baby girl at home lay sick unto death.

"Ah ha!" the devil tempted Billy. "It will take seven pounds to cover the chapel and you have only two. Your baby is going to die. It will take one pound to bury her and then you'll have only one pound left. It would have been better never to have started the chapel than to have to quit before it's finished. What a laughingstock you will be!"

But Billy put his case in the Lord's hands. It was for his Father that he was building the chapel, and the outcome was up to Him. While Billy prayed, a strong conviction rested upon him that he would be paid for building the chapel. Said the Lord, "Because thou hast built this chapel, I will save the child's life."

Billy went home and told Joey.

"The child will not die, but live," he announced joyfully, "the Lord has told me so."

"Ah! Billy!" Joey shook her head, "don't speak foolishly. All the neighbors say she must die. She is so ill, Billy. Look at her. So very ill."

All that day the child grew worse. All that night she hung between life and death. The next morning she grew no better. After dinner Billy knelt down with his family before going to the mines to work.

"Dear Lord," he prayed, "Thou hast said that my child shall live, but she has not eaten anything yet . . ."

Just then there was a stirring in the bed improvised on the windowseat, and the sound of sobbing. Joey hurried to the little girl's side, took her up, and gave her baked potato softened with milk and butter. She ate there and then, and lived to grow up to become eventually the mother of ten children.

"Once more," said Billy, "the Lord has made the devil out a liar."

This incident made Billy even more bold in his asking, and in due time the money he needed to finish the building was forthcoming. Finally the chapel was completed. Billy named it Bethel. He was well repaid for all his labor and struggle, as, in the years ensuing, the work of the Lord revived in that place, and as many as fifty at one time alone knelt and found mercy at the altar he had made with his own hands. Later, by the same method of faith and perseverance, he built a chapel at Kerley Downs, and yet another at Gwennap.

Upon the completion of the chapel at Kerley Downs, Billy began looking around for a pulpit. One day at an auction sale, his eye fell upon an old three-cornered cupboard.

"Just the thing!" cried Billy, "the very thing! I know exactly how it can be fixed into as pretty a pulpit as a preacher ever preached from."

He turned to a man beside him. "What do you think they'll want for that cupboard?" Billy asked with high anticipation.

"Why, around six shillings, I guess. What do you want it for?"

"A pulpit," Billy replied eagerly, "a pulpit for Kerley Downs Chapel."

"Oh, you're Billy Bray, aren't you?" interposed the man. "Here, I'll give you six shillings to buy it."

Soon the cupboard was offered for sale. Knowing nothing of auctions, Billy held out his hand to the auctioneer. "Here, Mister," he shouted, "here's six shillings for it. I want it for a pulpit."

"Six shillings," cried the auctioneer, "going for six."

But someone behind Billy nodded his head, and before Billy knew what was happening, the auctioneer called out, "Seven shillings. Going for seven."

"No," protested Billy, it's only six. Here. Here's the money."

But no amount of pleading could win him his point. The cupboard went to the other man.

"Well," conceded Billy in a rather disappointed tone, "my Father knows best. But how shall I give back the man his six shillings? He's gone and I know not where."

This dilemma troubled Billy even more than the loss of the cupboard, so he went to the chapel to pray about it. Just as he was leaving, having received the assurance that everything would be all right, he saw the cupboard going up the hill in a cart.

"Well," Billy whispered to himself, "just believe I'll follow it and see where it goes."

When they reached their destination, the men unloaded the cupboard and proceeded to carry it into the house, but lo! the doorway was too narrow. They maneuvered and pushed, they twisted and pulled, but to no avail.

"Now I am in for it," exclaimed the buyer impatiently. "Here I gave seven shillings for it and all I can do is cut it up for firewood!" He wiped his forehead dejectedly.

"Tell you what I'll do," Billy proposed, his eyes twinkling, as he put his hand on the man's shoulder. "I'll give you six shillings for it if you'll haul it down to my little chapel."

"It's a bargain!" agreed the man instantly, so gratified was he to come out of his difficulty so well.

"Bless the Lord!" cried Billy. "He knew I had no way to get the cupboard to the chapel myself, so he got you to haul it for me. It's just like my Father in Heaven!"

One of Billy Bray's most outstanding characteristics was his joyousness of spirit. He had trials just as everyone else does, but he did not think it worthwhile to speak or write of them. Said he, "I have a heaven while going to heaven. Should I not then praise God every step of the way?"

Once in a meeting, he gave out the first line of the hymn reading —

"Oh, for a thousand tongues to sing"

"Just think of it!" he paused, "that's nine hundred and ninety-nine more than I've got! Many of you don't sing with the one tongue you have, and object when Billy tries to use the one he has. But if Wesley wanted nine hundred and ninety-nine tongues more than he had, it is a hard thing if Billy cannot use his one."

Praising the Lord was one of Billy's favorite methods of fighting the devil. While he was walking home from revival meeting one dark night on a lonely road, some wild boys tried to silence his singing and shouting by making terrifying, unearthly sounds. Paying no attention, Billy walked on, singing as before.

Perturbed at his nonchalance, one of the ruffians boomed, "But I'm the devil up here in the hedge, Billy Bray. Didn't you know that?"

"Bless the Lord! Bless the Lord!" shouted Billy, "I didn't know you were so far away as that!"

It was Billy's belief that in keeping small and lowly at the feet of Jesus he was safeguarded from the enemy. "Soon after I was converted," he confided once, "the devil said to me, 'Billy Bray, you'll be a great man someday,' but I sunk into nothing, and in that way slipped through the devil's hands."

Billy Bray, extraordinary in his life of faith and praise, was born near Truro, Cornwall, England, on June 1, 1794. His early years were spent in wild orgies of drunkenness and mischief, but when God in His mercy awakened him to righteousness, the change was sudden and decisive. From this time on he became one of the most effective witnesses for God and righteousness ever known.

He was a small, wiry man with a discerning eye and a face softened by light emanating from his very soul. The happy smile that had established itself as indeed belonging to his countenance, bespoke the heavenly joy that constantly abode within. He liked to refer to himself as "The King's son," and as such he trusted implicitly in the King for every need. He invested in the Kingdom's work so nearly all the money he could earn in the mines that he and his family clothed themselves almost entirely with garments others gave them.

Once a friend approached Billy and said, "Here, neighbor, the Lord told me to give you a coat and waistcoat. Try them on. Don't know whether they'll fit you or not."

"Fit me?" returned Billy in wonder, "If the Lord told you to give them to me, they will fit me all right. He knows my size exactly. Besides, you know, fashion and I quarreled once, and we've never made up."

Even to old age, Billy, like his Master, "went about doing good." His greetings to friend and stranger alike took the form of wise and pointed questions about the state of their souls. And if the answers were what they should be, the countryside would ring with his praises to God. He took long journeys visiting the sick and ministering to their heart needs. He held frequent services, fasted, prayed, and praised, seeing glorious victories won for God. To the very end, which came when he was seventy-four years of age, his passion to see benighted ones saved was a living fire in his breast. To the end his praises ceased not. His last breath was spent in shouting "glory," and with that, leaving behind him a trail of eternal glory, he entered the land of eternal splendor — of glory evermore.

A Flicker of Candlelight

YOUNG HUDSON TAYLOR stepped out of his aunt's pleasant home with the exhilaration of daring purpose in his stride. Ah! This was life! What could equal the thrill of venturing upon God? Of proving Him to be the One He promises to be?

Leaving behind him the cultured, residential area of Hull, England, the lad wended his way to the outskirts of town. Then, following a muddy trail past several vacant lots, he came upon the double row of cottages for which he was looking. They bordered a narrow canal, used by the surrounding inhabitants as a rubbish dump, which accounted for the name of "Drainside" being given to the unsightly neighborhood. The poor, little dwellings were all alike, boasting of only one door and two windows apiece, so that young Hudson could not have been sure which was the object of his quest except for the hand-printed sign in one window.

"Room for rent," it announced simply.

He went in, and scarcely stopping to survey his new quarters, paid the landlady for a month's rent. Adjusting his few belongings to the stinted accommodations afforded him, he set about preparing his evening meal, a little awkwardly perhaps, but with a low-whistled tune on his lips and a new warm light in his eye.

He knew he would miss the cheer of his aunt's hospitable home, the satisfying goodness of her well-cooked meals, the comfort of her fellowship, but such things would not make a man of him. At least, the kind of man he intended to be. So now, he was voluntarily leaving it all behind, leaving it to steel himself to hardship, leaving it to prepare himself for the rigor of missionary work in China.

Having partaken of his simple meal, Hudson Taylor stood long at the window, its view opening upon the odious canal ditch, the dingy row of shacks, the poverty rampant everywhere.

109

"Why should I live better than they?" he asked the silence that enveloped him, and realized he had raised a question to which there was no answer.

A few evenings later, this same youth, in the same dreary room, sat down with pencil and paper. His salary was adequate enough, for he served as assistant to a leading physician in Hull, a Doctor Hardy by name. But the figuring showed that young Hudson was comparing prices of foods, estimating how much he could save by eating rice and oatmeal instead of meat, milk and butter. The result of his study was gratifying. By denying self he could save more than two-thirds of his income. And why this frugality? So that, beyond his accustomed tithing, he would have more to give to the destitute and starving not only here at his door, but in all the poorer quarters of town where he had been regularly evangelizing.

Not long after this, young Taylor was arrested by another challenge. *When I get to China*, he thought to himself, *I shall have no claim on anyone for anything. There will be no Doctor Hardy there giving me monthly wages. My only claim will be on God. How important it is then that I shall learn, before leaving my homeland, to move man, through God, by prayer alone.*

It was a great ambition, but how should he begin? The answer came almost immediately, suggested by Doctor Hardy as the two parted one evening.

"I say, Taylor," the doctor admonished him pleasantly, "be sure to remind me when your salary comes due. There are absent-minded doctors, you know, as well as absent-minded professors."

The young assistant smiled but made no promises.

"Here is my chance," the youth concluded secretly, when the doctor had turned to go. "Instead of reminding him directly that payday has come, I will ask God to bring the fact to his attention. I will see what can be done in answer to prayer. Thus shall my faith be encouraged for all my needs as missionary in the future."

In due time, the day drew near for another payment of salary. Young Taylor prayed much. The day came and went, however, without Doctor Hardy so much as mentioning the matter. More prayer ascended, and more time elapsed without the doctor remembering.

"Foolish man!" taunted the accuser of men's souls, "You don't need to pinch and sacrifice. And to pray that God will remind the doctor that your pay is due, is like tempting the Almighty. You have tongue and breath. Remind him yourself!"

It sounded reasonable. But it was not the money that distressed Hudson Taylor, and he told the tempter so. "See here," he said, and in the saying added new fuel to the fire burning within, "my face is set for China. There I must trust God for every need. But if I have not the faith to prove Him here, how can I there? The test is on. Can I go to China, or can I not? Will my faith and power with God in prayer prove of sufficient strength or will my lack of it prohibit my entering upon this much-prized service?"

That was the question. And Hudson Taylor continued to pray.

As another week drew to a close and no mention had yet been made of his salary, the prospective missionary faced not only his own dire paucity, but his obligation to his landlady, who was indeed as penniless as himself. The test grew severe, but he committed the thing to God, believing that in some way or other He would interpose on his behalf.

Saturday dawned, counted out its hours to a work-a-day world, then gave way to the shadows of twilight. The rent was due that night. When Doctor Hardy had finished writing his prescriptions, he threw himself back in his armchair and began to talk to Hudson about the things of God, as he was truly a Christian man.

Hudson entered into the conversation eagerly as he had done so many times before, and a precious time of fellowship ensued, the young assistant continuing all the while to watch a pan in which a decoction was boiling which required a good deal of attention.

Suddenly, without any obvious connection with the subject being discussed, the doctor inquired, "By the by, Taylor, is not your salary due again?"

Hudson's spoon stopped its stirring for a split second. He swallowed once, convulsively, then again. But with his eye fixed on the pan and his back to the doctor, he managed to say quite calmly, "Why, yes, doctor, it is. In fact, I believe it has been overdue for some time."

It was with some difficulty that he retained even a semblance of composure. "Praise God!" he breathed inwardly. "He has surely heard my prayer and caused my employer in this time of my great extremity, to remember my salary, without a word from me!"

But the doctor was talking again. "Oh, I am so sorry you did not remind me. You know how busy I am. I wish I had thought of it a little sooner, for only this afternoon I sent all the money I had to the bank. Otherwise, I would pay you at once."

Again the assistant's spoon stopped stirring, and when, at that moment, the pan boiled up, young Hudson concealed the shock that had so nearly floored him by rushing with the hot solution from the room.

In a few minutes, the doctor made his way through the garden to his dwelling house, and the lad left behind sought a little sanctum where he could pour out his heart to the Lord. As the evening wore on, calmness again possessed the heart so taken in a moment by crushing disappointment, and Hudson, contenting himself that surely Monday morning he should be able to pay his landlady, diligently studied the sermon he planned to preach in the various lodging houses on the morrow. When the clock struck ten, he put on his overcoat, and was turning down the gas, when lo! he heard the doctor's step in the garden. This was strange, he thought, and stranger still, the doctor was laughing!

"Where's my ledger, Taylor?" the physician asked, stepping in the door. "One of my richest patients has just paid his bill! Can you imagine that? At this time of night! An odd thing, an odd thing, indeed!" He chuckled again, shaking his head, nonplussed.

Hudson, too, laughed heartily. To think of a man rolling in wealth not being able to find rest of mind until he came after ten o'clock at night to pay a bill he could have met any day by check, seemed almost absurd. But so it was. Perhaps it was stranger still that the young man so in need of money did not associate the incident with himself until Doctor Hardy, about to leave the office, suddenly turned and handed him some of the bills just received.

"By the by, Taylor," he said unexpectedly, "you might as well take this much. I can give you the balance next week."

Hudson stood transfixed for many moments watching the doctor disappear into the night. Then, dropping to his knees he breathed rather than spoke the joy of his heart.

"To think," he whispered, when he had regained some composure, "to think that I may go to China after all!"

To China Hudson Taylor most certainly went.

At twenty-one years of age he was wrested from his studies in medicine and surgery to answer a frantic call for workers, and after a perilous voyage of five months' duration, he found himself precipitated into war-torn Shanghai. Famine prices prevailed, and as coal was selling for fifty dollars a ton, little could be done to battle the bitter winter weather. So stiffened by cold that he could hardly hold a pen, Hudson Taylor had cause to rejoice that he had not pampered himself with luxuries in America, so that now he was truly able to thank God for any kind of shelter.

In spite of the language barrier, constant war, and unthinkable deprivations, the young missionary made no fewer than ten evangelistic journeys inland by waterway during his first two years in China. From the outset, his heart was set on reaching the millions of the "interior," and to facilitate his message being favorably received by the people, he very soon adopted native dress. On many of his missions he was companionless, feeling his loneliness keenly, but no sacrifice detained him. Indeed, such a thing as sacrifice completely eluded his thinking. In later years he wrote, "I never sacrificed anything."

Trying to work his way inland, the new missionary once found a temporary home in the dispensary of a Doctor Parker in the city of Ningpo. Here he traced his initials on the snow which collected on his coverlet by night, thanking God for a place to settle where he found ample scope for service, both medical and evangelistic, morning, noon, and night. Little could he imagine then that the barnlike upper room which comprised his quarters at that time would one day be remodeled and used as the first station of the China Inland Mission. But so it was to be.

For six years the valiant missionary pushed on in his ever widening mission of faith. Then illness forced him, for five long years, to leave his beloved work. Invalided home with his young wife in 1860, at the age of twenty-nine, his battles against an impatient and murmuring spirit would have prostrated a less courageous soul. But Hudson Taylor, knowing that God had a purpose even in this, sought to find that purpose, meanwhile filling his days with any service at hand. During this time, he revised the Chinese New Testament, and, after much spiritual agony, answered God's call to accept the leadership of new recruits for China, a responsibility he had long shrank from, one of much more serious import than merely praying workers out to the field.

Setting out as the leader of a party of sixteen missionaries and four children, Hudson Taylor rested in the assurance that God is sufficient for God's own work. The great desire and aim of each of his party was to plant the standard of the cross in the eleven provinces of China hitherto unoccupied, and in Chinese Tartary.

One of the mission's most generous supporters in ensuing days proved to be a man in England as penniless as Hudson Taylor himself. George Mueller, already by prayer and by faith providing for some two thousand orphan children, donated to the work in China nearly ten thousand dollars annually, over a period of several years.

At one time, when funds were so low that he scarcely knew how to distribute the little that did come in, the dauntless missionary asked God for fifty or one hundred additional native evangelists and as many missionaries as might be needed to open up the four provinces and forty-eight cities still unoccupied in Chekiang. Said he, "I long for this by day and pray for it by night. Can He care less?"

Just when advance had never seemed more impossible, and Taylor himself lay on his back in helpless suffering, a letter from an unkown correspondent in England promised him four thousand dollars for work in "fresh" provinces. At another time came three thousand pounds (over $14,000) in answer to his prayer for seventy new recruits and the means to send them out.

In similar ways other substantial gifts poured in, and workers were made available. In 1887, Taylor challenged the Christian world to pray for one hundred new recruits for China in one year, and $50,000 to send them out. Six hundred men and women actually offered themselves for the work that year, of whom one hundred two were chosen, and not $50,000 but $55,000 extra was actually received.

By the time Hudson Taylor lay down his work, he had a corps of seven hundred fifty missionaries and seven hundred Chinese workers. $4,000,000 had come into his hands for the spreading of the Gospel in China and 13,000 had been definitely converted to God.

Be it said of Hudson Taylor that not only in money matters did he find his Lord sufficient, but in every matter that concerned his life, not the least of these being in the area of sorrow and loneliness. The first blow to fall upon the man of God came in the death of his eight-year-old daughter at Hangchow in the torrid summer of 1867.

"Our dear little Gracie!" he wrote to his mother. "How we miss her sweet voice in the morning, one of the first sounds to greet us when we woke, and through the day and at eventide! As I take the walks I used to take with her tripping figure at my side, the thought comes anew like a throb of agony, 'Is it possible that I shall nevermore feel the pressure of that little hand . . . nevermore see the sparkle of those bright eyes?' And yet she is not lost."

To a friend he wrote, "It was no vain nor unintelligent act when, knowing this land, its people and climate, I laid my wife and children with myself on the altar for this service . . . He has not left us now."

Before a driving storm the parents crossed the river

Then came the time when they could no longer delay the inevitable parting from their children, who must needs go to far-away England for school privileges. Heartbreaking as was this prospect, a longer parting yet was to be faced even before the little travelers could be escorted to the coast. The youngest of the boys, an especially clinging little five-year-old, drooped and died on the boat that was taking the family down the turbid waters of the Yangtze. Before a driving storm, the parents crossed the river — there about two miles wide — to lay their treasure in the cemetery at Chinkiang, and then went on with the others to Shanghai.

That same summer their hearts were again to be torn by the

death of their new-born baby boy. And in a few days more, Hudson Taylor was called to suffer the supreme sorrow of his life, alone, for in August, his precious wife went to be with her Redeemer.

It was in the days of utter desolation which followed that the dauntless missionary found the words of a special promise made so real to his breaking heart.

"How lonesome were the weary hours when confined to my room," Mr. Taylor recalled later. "How I missed my dear wife and the voices of the children far away in England! Then it was I understood why the Lord had made that message so real to me, 'Whosoever drinketh of the water that I shall give him *shall never thirst.*' Twenty times a day, perhaps, as I felt the heart-thirst coming back, I cried to Him, 'Lord, You promised! You promised me that I should never thirst.' And whether I called by day or night, how quickly He came and satisfied my sorrowing heart! So much so that I often wondered whether it were possible that my loved one who had been taken could be enjoying more of His presence than I was in my lonely chamber."

For the secret of Hudson Taylor's victorious walk with God, and the success of his ventures for the Kingdom, a peep into the tiny curtained-off corner of a large room in one of Northern China's poorest inns, where travelers and coolies alike were wont to find shelter for the night, would have told us all. Thence his party had traveled by cart and wheelbarrow. Now, far into the night when the confusion had abated, and at last a measure of quiet had brought sleep to most of the sojourners, a match was struck. There was a flicker of candlelight. And the slight flutter of turning pages revealed that Mr. Taylor, weary though he must have been, was poring over his well-worn Bible. From two to four A.M., he read and wept and prayed. It was the only time he was most sure of being undisturbed as he waited upon God, and so it was not only a vigil of one night, but of every night.

Can one wonder that God used Hudson Taylor? The flicker of candlelight — a little thing. Yet it bespoke the tenor of the man's whole life — the sacrifices that started at Drainside, the prayer warfare that was born at the time of his conversion.

Said he, "There are not two Christs — an easy-going one for easy-going Christians, and a suffering, toiling one for exceptional believers. There is only one Christ. Are you willing to abide in *Him* and thus bear much fruit?"

"I Cannot Stop"

In a shack upon the hot sands of an island seashore off the coast of West Africa lay the figure of a young man. His body burned with fever hotter than the sands. He tossed in delirium and panted with thirst.

"Woman!" he cried piteously. "Water! Bring me water! Water! Wa-ter!"

An irresponsible, heartless female approached the wretch who was at her mercy.

"Don't know why I'm doing this," she grumbled half to herself and half to the victim, "for I care not whether you live or die. But if it'll stop your everlasting crying for me, here — "

She poured a few drops down the gasping man's throat and departed, to shut her ears to his disconcerting wails for another twenty-four hours or so.

How he survived those endless days and nights of unspeakable torment, misery and shocking neglect, John Newton never knew, except it be by the mercy of God.

In time, however, he awakened to the fact that his fever was gone and his hunger had risen almost to a frenzy. Still he lay at the mercy of this black one, his master's "woman." For his master was gone and would not return for weeks, perhaps.

"Woman!" John called till he could scarcely make a noise above a whisper, but there was no response. He cried like a baby — he, slave trader veteran of the high seas, tough. Could he, this blubbering, helpless castaway on the sands of Africa, be the same self-sufficient John Newton who had always considered himself as being in need of nothing? Unthinkable! But true.

"Woman!" he called again.

Ah! here she came!

"Take this," she snorted, as she shoved him a plate at arm's length. It was the same plate from which she herself had eaten, and contained a few morsels she had not wanted.

"Thank you, oh, thank you!" John repeated again and again.

So grateful was he for a swallow of something nourishing. So greatly had his pride been humbled!

Once his benefactress would not so much as stoop to put his dish upon his bed.

"Reach up and take it," she ordered roughly.

John attempted to do so, but was too feeble to hold the plate. It fell and broke in pieces at his side, the food scattering beyond his grasp.

John's disappointment was incomparable. With wordless entreaty his eyes besought the face of the woman for a crumb of pity if not of bread. But she only laughed, raucously, cruelly, and refused to give him another scrap, though her table was full.

When, incredibly, John's strength finally returned to the extent that he could crawl a short distance, he was compelled to drag himself around at night (though he risked being punished as a thief) to hunt roots which he ate raw to keep himself alive.

When his master at length returned — a slave trader into whose service John had previously been hired — the youth had so far regained his strength as to be able to embark on another journey.

Though the nameless torture thus recently suffered by John off the coast of Africa seems to have had no immediate effect upon the attitudes of his soul, it is hardly credible that an experience so nearly fatal should not bring upon him a sobering influence. For, in truth, at various times in the tenderness of his eighteen years, John had been so deeply moved upon religiously that he had spent the greater part of every day in reading the Scriptures, meditation and prayer, had fasted often, and had even refused to answer questions for fear of speaking an idle word.

Now he was as profligate as he had been virtuous. On the return voyage from Africa to England, he was so profane that the captain, anything but saintly himself, reproved him stoutly.

But God still had his hand upon John Newton. The youth was naturally a student. And when on shipboard he could find nothing more to his liking, he contented himself with reading *The Imitation of Christ* by Thomas a'Kempis, one of the few books available. At first his perusal was rather careless. But after reading the timeless classic again and again, he startled himself one day by asking, "What if these things should be true?" The question was a hard one — one he could not bear to ponder.

He closed the book, joined his comrades in shallow talk and laughter, and tried to force himself to forget.

That night, however, John was forced to *remember*. No sooner had he fallen to sleep than he was pitched from his bunk and rolled on the floor. Timbers creaked and groaned in a mighty storm. The sea broke violently over the deck and water soon filled his cabin. From the first, no one doubted that the ship and all on board would be lost.

"To the pumps! Man the pumps!" men were shouting everywhere.

John had already bounded to the hold. Brawny seamen worked heroically, almost superhumanly. In spite of frantic efforts, however, the water deepened with every minute. Providentially, their cargo consisted of beeswax and wood, both of them lighter than water, else the boat would have sunk in the blackness of night.

The next morning John went to the captain. Some of the water had been emptied from the ship and the leaks stopped.

"If this will not do," John said, nearly exhausted from hours of labor and exposure, "the Lord have mercy upon us!"

He stopped. His own words startled him. What had he said? "Mercy?" Then aloud, "*What mercy can there be for me?*"

He went back to the pumps. On and on he toiled, almost every wave breaking over his head. Surely in one of these deluges the ship must go under!

What can I do? thought he, half sullenly. *I'm caught! Yes, caught! A ghastly predicament indeed! For life there is no hope. To die I am afraid! That there is mercy, I am only half convinced. Oh, what a mixture of despair and impatience! How will it end? How?*

At noon John was so exhausted he gave up, dropped on his bed, and little cared whether he ever woke up or not. In an hour he was called, however, and went to the helm. His reflections upon the state of his soul again monopolized his thinking.

"I've broken through such rare advantages," he reasoned to himself, "I've scorned the light and glory I once knew. I've trodden underfoot the blood of the Son of God. I've . . . Oh, surely there never was or could be such a sinner as myself! My sins are too great, too great to be forgiven!"

He struggled on, more like a machine than a man. About six in the evening, the ship was freed from water, but was so battered that the survival of its passengers was precarious indeed.

"Christ died for our sins that were not His own," John tried to assure himself. "But I have been an infidel so long. I find myself *wishing* the Gospel were true rather than *believing* it. Still, You have promised the Holy Spirit to them that ask Thee," he addressed the Lord, "I will ask Thee for Thy Spirit. And if the promise is true, Thou wilt make it good."

With this proposition, John took the Gospel at its word.

The wind had moderated by this time, but the ship and its sails were so wrecked that little hope of seeing land again was held. Provisions shrank to such scanty proportions that the crew were almost too weak to man the pumps properly. For four weeks this hazardous plight prevailed, when at last the little boat and its occupants arrived at Lough Swilly in Ireland. Their deliverance had come none too soon, for at that moment their "last victuals were boiling in the pot," and two hours later such a storm whipped the sea that if their little vessel, already pounded and broken, had been at its mercy, it would have perished for sure.

"Now I begin to know of a certainty," confessed young John, "that there is a God who hears and answers prayer."

It was the turning point in John Newton's life. Profoundly grateful for the undeserved mercy shown him in his being brought safely through so many dangers, he repented of his wicked ways and heartily renounced them all, finding immediate deliverance from the habit of profanity which seemed to have been as deeply rooted in him as second nature. It was, indeed, the beginning as John said, "of my return to God, or rather of *His* return to me . . ."

Even after his conversion, John continued for several years in the slave trade, commanding several ships voyaging in this business. Eventually, however, he was so convinced of its evils that, said he, "I asked God to fix me in a more humane calling. . . . Custom, example, and interest had blinded my eyes. I did it ignorantly."

God did "fix" him in a more humane calling, that of preaching the Gospel, but for this he was compelled to tarry most patiently. Appointed to the post of Tide Surveyor of the port of Liverpool, he had leisure time at his command, which he redeemed by church-going, study, prayer and meditation. During these years he sought out God's will as to whether he should enter the ministry. Even after he had made the final decision to consider himself "as torn off from the world and worldly concerns, and devoted and appointed for sanctuary service," he was to wait six years more for his ordination. Finally in 1764, at the age of thirty-nine years, he was presented with the Curacy of Olney.

Surely here John followed in the footsteps of our Saviour who said of his own ministry, "the poor have the Gospel preached to them." This "little, odd-looking man" went in and out the streets of his parish, wearing his blue sea jacket which he preferred to the clerical garb of the Anglican church, bringing cheer to the sick, comforting the lonely, witnessing to the good mercy of the Lord upon himself — "a wild beast on the coast of Africa" . . . whom "the Lord caught . . . and tamed," — and, in short, shepherding with a great heart of love his poor needy sheep.

Olney was populated by the "half-starved and ragged of the earth." Noted for its lace making, its women labored ten and twelve hours a day, its children almost as long, in rooms crowded, poorly heated, and ill lighted — one candle to every three or four workers — for only a mere pittance with which to keep soul and body together. Especially did the pastor's heart go out to the children, these mere babes toiling so pitifully beyond their years. When he saw one whose heart had been broken, a child who had dropped a halfpenny perhaps, "if, by giving it another," said John, "I can wipe away the tears, I feel I have done something."

He explained the Scriptures to them "in their own little way"

No wonder that a man who felt that such small kindnesses were worth his time, should be able to gather around him eighty-nine children in his first children's meeting, the number exceeding two hundred in the months that followed. He taught them the catechism to be sure, but that was not all. He talked, he preached, reasoned with them and explained the Scriptures to them "in their own little way." John's work with the children was a forerunner of that of men like Robert Raikes, who later founded the Sunday school.

Besides the children's work, John applied himself to the interests of the young people, to prayer and Bible study groups. It is said that a constant stream of hungry souls came to hear him preach or to talk with him privately about their problems. In Olney, it came to be a difficult matter to find anyone who made no profession of religion at all. So conscientious, sacrificing and faithful was John Newton in the service of his Lord. His godly life and preaching greatly influenced William Cowper, the poet of the Evangelical Party, and Thomas Scott, a minister in the Church of England, who in turn influenced William Carey, later the father of modern missions.

John composed hymns for his own services and to him are we indebted for that matchless expression not only of his, but of our own soul's cry,

> Amazing grace! (how sweet the sound)
> That sav'd a wretch like me!
> I once was lost, but now am found,
> Was blind, but now I see.

When, in 1779, John moved from his parish in Olney to one in London, he found himself among the wealthy, but even here he was never happier than when out seeking the poor.

His one obsession was the spread of the Gospel. Always at it, he never took a vacation without managing to preach somewhere. Always, in season, out of season, he bore witness to the saving power of Jesus Christ. Henry Martyn profited from John's excellent spiritual advice. Charles Wesley thought so much of this devoted follower of the Saviour that he requested him to be one of the pall bearers at his funeral. He was an instrument in Wilberforce's conversion, and, ironically, Wilberforce in turn became an instrument in abolishing the slave trade — the trade so long indulged in by John himself before his awakening to its evil.

Even when overtaken by old age and handicapped by deafness, blindness and a failing memory, John maintained the same aggression for the cause of Christ. He preached whenever he had half a chance. But would it not be better to "stop before you . . . discover you can speak no longer?" someone approached him one day.

"Stop?" exclaimed the aged veteran, "I cannot stop. What! Shall the old African blasphemer stop while he can speak?"

Nor did John Newton stop until death itself caught up with him at the age of eighty-three. And though at that time the voice grew silent, the works of this subject of amazing grace do follow him, to help us on to God.

The Apostle of the Open Road

JOHN WESLEY WAS IN LONDON when he first heard of the outrages in Staffordshire.

"Nearly every Methodist house has its windows broken out," the word came. "Furniture is demolished. Burned. Tradesmen's shops are gutted. Men have been beaten senseless and kicked into gutters. Crazed mobs have even threatened to murder the women and girls. Already they've injured some by throwing stones at them, or beating them with clubs."

Such violences were not new to Wesley, but he had not expected them in the villages of Staffordshire. As the leader of these Methodists, Wesley was fearless for himself, but solicitious in the extreme for the safety of his sheep. He hurried to the spot. Strangely enough, he preached in the marketplace at high noon without opposition. Within a couple of hours, however, his opponents had raised a mob. Before it was over, they dragged the preacher through the streets of their town and showered him with stones. A vicious rascal forced his way through the mob. He raised his brutal arm to strike Wesley. Then suddenly he let it drop, and only stroked the good man's head.

"What silky hair he has," he said unexpectedly.

All at once the mob became powerless to harm the fearless little preacher. The captain of the rogues, a prize fighter, stood before Wesley.

"Sir, I will spend my life for you," he said meekly. "Follow me and not one soul here shall touch a hair of your head."

"In all that uproar," Wesley told his brother the next day, "I lost only a flap of my waistcoat, and a little skin from off my hand. Praise be unto God!"

It was not long until the prize fighter joined one of the societies which Wesley had organized to encourage and nurture his converts in the Christian way. He remained a loyal Methodist until his death fifty years later.

"What do you think of my brother?" Charles Wesley asked him one day.

"Think of him!" roared the ex-fighter. "Why, sir, that he is a mon of God. And God was on his side sure, when so many of us could not kill one mon!"

At Yarmouth, while Wesley was preaching in the market-place, a policeman came up and said sternly, "You must move on, you must move on!"

Wesley smilingly replied, "Oh, I can easily do that. I am a traveling preacher." And the whole crowd laughingly followed him!

Such were some of the forces arrayed against John Wesley, founder of Methodism, as he took to the open road to preach salvation from all sin to eighteenth-century England. Perhaps his courage and fortitude stemmed no more from certain inherent characteristics than they did from certain boyhood experiences with England's lower classes. Indeed, from them he expected nothing better than what he now witnessed, perhaps. Had they not shown their animosity toward the plain preaching of his father by stabbing three of the family's cows in the good man's absence, then had finished their malicious intent by cutting the watchdog's leg nearly off? And who could say that the burning of the Epworth parsonage was not the outgrowth of the same spiteful spirit? It was with this almost fatal fire in mind that Wesley often referred to himself as "a brand plucked from the burning."

Such experiences had taught Wesley to pursue life and his God-given purposes with noble disregard for the persecutions of others and the adverseness of circumstances. Thus, when he had accepted Governor Oglethorpe's proposition to go to America and preach to the Indians in Georgia, though he felt afterward that his mission had been largely in vain, every settler in the new colony, in addition to many African slaves and Indians, heard the Gospel from John Wesley's lips. And all this was accomplished in spite of almost unthinkable privations.

It was during this mission that he became deeply conscious of a lack in his own Christian experience. First, there had been the tempest at sea which threatened to sink the ship and all the souls aboard. Wesley had joined a group of Moravians in their public devotions, and when in the storm an immense wave broke over the ship just as they were singing their evening song, he was struck with wonder that they lost not a single note. The English passengers screamed in terror, but the Moravians sang on, as calmly as though they had been in their own chapel in Herrnhut.

It was this deep and quiet faith of the Moravian company that caused Wesley to covet a like experience in his own heart — an experience he felt he could not attain.

One May evening after his return to England, his heart still torn with nameless longing, he wandered into an Aldersgate Street prayer meeting where Luther's preface to the book of Romans was being read. The words repeated what the Moravians in America had tried to explain to him — how God changes the heart through faith in Christ. Suddenly, the truth and simplicity of it all burst in upon his consciousness and John Wesley felt his heart strangely warmed — warmed and filled with the presence of God Himself.

It was a turning point in his life. From that time forward, his ministry began to leave its stamp for righteousness upon all phases of English life. And now, his unceremonious ministry in the open air, though sometimes thwarted by brutal mobs, led to an itineracy of preaching that reached tens of thousands of people.

For years on end, the torrid days of summer, the beautiful days of fall, and the stormy days of winter — all of them — found Wesley and his steed on their way to a neglected group of people somewhere who would be waiting to hear the indefatigable little preacher speak to them of eternal things. Winters in England were bitter and the roads, scarcely more than winding, muddy trails, often were well nigh impassable.

It was an exceptionally bleak morning when Wesley, on one of his journeys, opened his eyes in the dark of a frigid room in a poor inn where he had taken lodging. He had felt faint and ill the day before, but now, refreshed and rested, he lighted his candle. Three o'clock. Without hesitation he jumped out of his none too comfortable bed into the icy atmosphere of the unheated room. True, he usually rose at four, but three was so much the better.

For an hour he prayed and read his Bible. Then he went to the stable and fed and bridled his steed. The weather had changed from a breathless cold to a full-blown storm. Wesley led his faithful comrade of the road out into the dark, shut the stable door behind them, sprang into the saddle and they were off.

Hail drove into their faces so sharply they could hardly breathe

Hail drove into their faces so sharply that they could hardly breathe. The rider pulled his waistcoat collar high around his chin and encouraged the horse with gentle words. All morning they pushed on, reaching Baldock at two, and, guided thence by a companion, they arrived in Patten at six. There Wesley preached to a serious congregation in a poorly heated room. Chilled to the bone, he and his guide went to bed in a cold, cheerless nook upstairs.

If anything, the next day was worse. The horses could scarcely keep their footing as they ploughed through the unbroken snow in the choking wind. During the day the snow changed to hail and rain, which drove through clothing and boots, freezing as it fell. When finally they reached the inn at Stilton, men and beasts had scarcely strength or ability of motion left. However, after a breathing spell, off they started again through drifts that almost swallowed them up.

The next day Wesley's companion was ready to stay where they were until the weather moderated. "Why, the roads are quite filled up and impassable," he remonstrated. "It is foolish to consume our strength in such a useless endeavor."

But Wesley was not content to stay. "At least we can walk twenty miles a day leading our horses behind us," he replied cheerfully.

So, in the name of God they pushed on in a northwest wind "that was as piercing as a sword."

"But do you not feel like quitting sometimes or at least resting on days like this?" his companion asked him.

"You remind me of a woman who couldn't help telling me how sorry she felt that I should have left all my friends to lead such a vagabond life as this," said Wesley. "I told her that indeed it was not pleasing to flesh and blood, and I would rather not do it, if I did not believe there was another world."

And so, with this thought always impelling him, Wesley pressed on.

For fifty-two years he ordered his days so as to include in them as much service for God as possible. For fifty-two years he preached in jails, graveyards, horse fairs, mining pits, inns, private houses, the open fields, the valleys, on the hillsides and the street corners. For a whole week he preached on his father's tombstone. He preached in sunshine and rain, cold and heat, darkness and light, to large crowds and small.

"Where is your most remarkable preaching location?" Dr. Samuel Johnson, a close friend of the family, once asked Wesley.

The good man reflected a moment. "There are several good ones," he mused. Then he turned to Dr. Johnson in an animated mood. "There is one that God must have made just for the purpose of outdoor preaching. Have you ever been at Gwennap in Cornwall?" He did not wait for an answer. "Well do I remember my last visit there. The evening was calm and still with the sun setting behind me. An immense multitude faced me. Besides those who filled the gigantic amphitheater, there were many sitting on little hills some distance away. And I don't think one of them missed a word!"

Wesley chuckled as he remembered.

"Think of it! Just think of it, Samuel! An old man of seventy being heard by thirty thousand people at once! Ah! it is one of the most magnificent spectacles to be seen this side of heaven."

He rose to his feet. "And no music is to be heard on earth comparable to the sound of many thousand voices when they are all harmoniously joined together singing praises to God and to the Lamb!"

Wesley walked back and forth in the room.

"Yes, yes, go on," urged Dr. Johnson, "tell me more. That is not all."

"No, it is not all," agreed Wesley, "God has done so much. At St. Ives I preached within sound of the sea from a pulpit formed by the natural rock. Well nigh the whole town, high and low, rich and poor, assembled together. I was afraid on

Saturday that the roaring of the sea, raised by the north wind, would prevent their hearing. But God gave me voice so clear and strong that I believe scarce one word was lost.

"Yes, and at Stonesey Gate," he chuckled, "I had a most astonishing open-air service. A very large congregation filled both the yard and the road to a considerable distance; and many were seated on a long wall adjoining, which being built of loose stones, in the middle of the sermon all fell down at once. I never saw, heard, nor read of such a thing before. The whole wall and the persons sitting upon it, sunk down together, none of them screaming out, and very few altering their posture. And not one was hurt at all; but they appeared sitting at the bottom just as they sat at the top. Nor was there any interruption either of my speaking, or of the attention of the hearers. Where can that be paralleled?"

The speaker had almost forgotten his friend, and like the aged man he was, he had been reveling in those wonderful experiences of the past. But even in this he could not indulge long. The open road was calling — calling.

"I must be going," he said abruptly.

Dr. Johnson started to remonstrate, but he knew it was of no use.

Wesley took his hat and cape from the wooden door peg, gathered up his satchel of books and was off again.

Dr. Johnson sat for a long moment in disappointed silence. "John Wesley's conversation is good," he said honestly to himself, "but he is never at leisure. He is always obligated to go at a certain hour. This is very disagreeable to a man who loves to fold his legs and have a talk out, as I do."

He rose from his chair and watched the preacher and his horse depart for points unknown.

"But his legs are not like mine," he commented to the empty room. "More than anywhere else, his legs are happier astride a horse on their way to a meeting!"

Dr. Johnson was not the only one who wished that Wesley would not hurry away. Everywhere the man of God went now, people begged for more of his words of counsel, wisdom and inspiration. Only in keeping on the move, however, could he reach so many people.

Did Wesley ever rest? Yes, according to his own testimony. Following a long and arduous tour of nearly seven months in all parts of the north of England and Ireland, suffering storms at sea and stress on every hand, he says, "I now rested a week at Bristol, preaching only morning and evening."

In those fifty-two years, Wesley traveled two hundred fifty thousand miles on land, and never less than forty-five hundred miles in any year. This was when there were no turnpikes in the north of England, and the London stagecoaches did not run beyond York. In June, 1751, he was nearly twenty hours in the saddle in one day and covered ninety miles. When he was sixty-three, his friends gave him a carriage and a pair of horses. He nailed up one side of his coach and built in shelves which he filled with books. He also included a board which could be let down to serve as a desk. All in one he had an office, a study, a bookshop, a library and a private chapel.

It was in this manner that Wesley made periodic visits to all the Methodist societies in England, counseling and nurturing his sheep wherever he went.

The more than six decades of Wesley's ministry yielded a varied store of experiences. Face to face with the devil most of the time, Wesley held his ground tenaciously, and, in the name of God, saw many a soul delivered from hell's mighty grip.

One evening he felt "exceedingly pressed" to go to a young woman in Kingswood. She was on her bed, apparently on the brink of eternity, but with anguish, horror and despair twisting her pale face. "The thousand distortions of her whole body," says Wesley, "showed how the dogs of hell were gnawing her heart. The shrieks intermixed were scarce to be endured. But her stony eyes could not weep."

Held down by two or three persons, she screamed out as soon as her paroxysms ceased, "I am damned, damned! lost forever! Six days ago you might have helped me. But it is past! I am the devil's now. With him I must go to hell. I cannot be saved. I will not be saved. I must, I will, I will be damned!"

Trusting to break the infernal spell, Wesley and his group began singing,
"Arm of the Lord, awake, awake!"
Immediately the young woman sunk back as though she had fallen asleep. But when the song ceased, she broke out again with "inexpressible vehemence," as though warning other lost souls.

"Stony hearts, break!" she screamed, "I am a warning to you. Break, break, poor stony hearts! You need not be damned, though I must."

She then fixed her eyes on the corner of the ceiling. "There he is," she gasped, "Ay, there he is!" Then in a tone of utter abandonment and despair, "Come, devil, come. Take me away. I am yours. I will be yours. Take me away."

Interrupting the whole terrible scene, Wesley and his group called upon the Almighty, storming the very gates of heaven.

The victim sunk down on her bed as before.

Now, Charles Wesley entered the room, it being about nine o'clock in the evening. And, in a situation which would have caused most men to despair or to flee, he and his brother battled the spirits of darkness until after eleven. By pleading the blood and declaring their faith in a God mightier than all the forces of evil, they saw the chains of darkness shatter! They saw a demon-possessed soul delivered in a moment of time! And the tongue which had so shortly before pleaded for the devil to take her away, now sang praises to God who had "stilled the enemy and the avenger."

With almost staggering accomplishments to his credit, Wesley however, never trusted in these for his own final acceptance with God. He once said, "I have been reflecting on my past life. I have been wandering up and down between fifty and sixty years, endeavoring in my poor way to do a little good to my fellow creatures, and now it is probable there are but a few steps between me and death, and what have I to trust to for salvation? I can see nothing which I have done or suffered that will bear looking at. I have no other plea than this, "I the chief of sinners am. But Jesus died for me!"

It seemed that England could not afford to lose the tireless efforts of such a man, but cease they must, at some time. A bit of pathos creeps into one of his journal entries toward the close of Wesley's life.

"I am eighty-six today," he wrote, "and I must admit that for nearly three years I have not been able to write more than fifteen hours a day without these poor eyes hurting me. And now I cannot easily preach more than twice a day. Besides, I lie in bed too long. Indeed, it was five-thirty this morning before I awoke. Such a habit must not take hold upon me! There is work to do. There is God's message to take! I live among multitudes who are creatures of only a day, passing through life as an arrow through the air. We are spirits come from God and returning to God; just hovering over the great gulf; till a few moments hence, we are no more seen! We drop into an unchangeable eternity!"

It was this awful consciousness of eternity that had projected Wesley from many a comfortable fireside into a cold, unfriendly England to save its masses from everlasting doom. The price was not paid in vain. Even in his lifetime, though he waited long for it, Wesley's soul was heartened to behold an abundant harvest from his labors. Out of the highways and hedges of all his beloved land flocked a warmhearted multitude who counted it a privilege just to glimpse their spiritual father as he might be passing by. Indeed, at the very place, where, forty years before, he was taken prisoner by a howling mob, he now found the street through which he traveled lined from one end of the town to the other by "high and low, out of stark love and kindness, gaping and staring as if the king were going by."

At eighty-eight years of age, this apostle of the open road left the roads of England and took the one to heaven, leaving behind him thousands who, because of his ministry and life, would soon follow him thither; leaving behind him an influence, a leadership and teaching which was to shape the eternal destiny of multitudes unborn, both in England and America. We of today reap in joy because he sowed in tears and hardship, to reveal to his fellowmen what the salvation of Jesus Christ really means — true holiness of heart and life. The tomorrows will not forget him nor his message, for both are immortal. And the end is not yet.

"Here I Stand"

It was deep in the autumn of 1510 that Martin Luther set out for the chapel, Sancta Sanctorum. Though Rome had been a disappointment in all other respects, perhaps, thought Luther, this chapel might give him that for which he had been searching.

He had been told that it held a flight of twenty-eight steps, Pilate's staircase, miraculously transported from Jerusalem to Rome — the very steps which had led to Pilate's judgment hall in Jesus' day. To ascend these sacred steps on one's knees, it was said, would assure the forgiveness of all sins. Indeed, Pope Leo IV in the ninth century had promised remission of guilt nine years for every step a pilgrim would climb in this manner, provided, of course, that the pilgrim would repeat certain prayers as he went. Luther longed for the peace of soul that this meritorious act was promised to give.

He quickened his step. Could it be that this day his long quest was to be terminated in satisfaction? He recalled with a sigh the years of groping for the certainty of a conscience void of offense toward God and man, the years of begging on the streets of Madgeburg and Eisenach that he might secure an education and thereby learn the way to heaven. He remembered his begging later on the streets of Erfurt that he might bring food to the monastery which he had entered as a monk. Then, he lived again the more recent months of the summer just past. How hopefully he had accepted the appointment to accompany an agent of several monasteries on a mission to Rome. How hopefully then, in pursuing this mission, he had traveled those hundreds of miles by foot and by wagon from Wittenburg, Germany, where he had been lecturer in the university.

Across the Alps, unfriendly and rugged, through streams that were swollen, through swamps that were dismal, and under a burning Italian sun he had trudged. How his heart had leaped within him, when, from the summit of a hill, he had first glimpsed the domes and the spires of the Holy City! So transported had he been at this glorious sight that he had fallen on his face to the ground, and had exclaimed, "Hail, Holy Rome! Ah! Holy City, I salute thee!" When at last he had actually entered the sacred gate, his heart glowing with devout expectation, he had cried in ecstasy, "Blessed Rome! Thou city sanctified by the blood of the martyrs, blessed Rome!"

But his joy had been short-lived. The city whose fame had distinguished it as being the capital of Christendom, he had found to be, instead, the hub of vice and immorality. The seat of the pope who was supposed to represent Christ on earth, the city of which Luther had dreamed as being a city of saints, the city made sacred by the blood of the Christian martyrs — this city he had discovered to be soaked in wickedness and corruption.

But surely he was not to leave the storied metropolis without some reward for his seeking. Surely this chapel with its hallowed staircase and its far-famed virtues would make amends for the profligacy of all the rest . . .

Reaching the sanctuary, he stood amazed at the awesomeness that confronted him. Others had come before, and, in the solemn hush of reverence everywhere, Luther caught now and again the earnest undertone of their voices in prayer — pilgrims struggling up the hallowed stairway. In profound humility and with bowed head and heart, Luther joined them. On bended knee he dragged himself to the lowest step, and prayed. To the next he crept, and prayed.

Ah! thought he, if only I may be rid of sin, the weary miles, the shattered hopes, the toilsome crawl up a hundred steps, though as cruel as these twenty-eight promise to be, will seem as inconsequential as waters that soon pass away.

So on he climbed. But as he did so, the weight on his breast which he thought should have lessened, grew more ponderous.

"Why this frustration?" he groaned. "Why will not favor attend me?"

Then it was as though for the first time he permitted his ears to hear the words that had been thundering in his soul for attention all day.

"The just shall live by faith," they said, "The just shall live by faith."

It was not just a passing thought. The scripture Luther had read time and again in the book of Romans now resounded unceasingly and powerfully within him. He rose from the steps in amazement. He shuddered, and felt himself ashamed to see to what a depth superstition had plunged him. Determination seized him. He was done and done forever with climbing holy stairsteps on his knees. He was done and done forever with trying to save himself by good works. He rushed from the spot ashamed of his folly, and forthwith returned to Wittenburg.

Not long after this, Luther became professor of theology in the Wittenburg University. The struggles of his own soul had come to an end and he encouraged others to depend on Jesus only for salvation.

About this time, Pope Leo X conceived a wonderful plan. Having imbibed the spirit of the Renaissance in its love of art as well as in its paganism, his ambition was to build, like Constantine, a church that would outshine that of Solomon and all who came after him. Michael Angelo himself had furnished the blueprints. All that was needed now was money. Much money. How was he to get it? Ecclesiastical deceit was equal to the emergency as is evidenced by the scheme decided upon — the sale of indulgences, or, as they have been termed, "letters of credit upon heaven." Did a man have sins chalked up against him? Then have them remitted by the payment of money. Did a man want to enter into a forbidden marriage relationship, gratify a secret wicked desire, escape the penalty when the deed was done, procure for his relatives a quick release from purgatory? Then all he had to do was to drop his money into the box provided for it, and as surely as the money tinkled, release and remission would be obtained.

John Tetzel was one of the shining lights in this business of selling indulgences. In a grand procession through the streets of Juterbuch, a town four miles from Wittenburg, he captured the hearts of the people with his promises of sins remitted in exchange for money.

When Luther heard of the high-handed practice of this man, his pious soul flamed with righteous wrath.

"If God permits," he vowed, "I will make a hole in his drum!" And he did.

All Saints Day was drawing near. It was a day of feasting, when crowds flocked to the church which Frederick had built in Wittenburg. The Elector had filled it with relics ornamented with gold, silver, and precious stones. These were exhibited to the people, and whoever visited the church at this time, making his confession, received a rich indulgence.

Luther bode his time. Then, at high noon, on October 31, 1517, the day before the feast, as multiplied throngs entered the church, he stepped up to the entrance and nailed ninety-five theses on the wooden door. Three of them were:

He stepped up to the entrance and nailed 95 theses on the wooden door

"They preach mere human follies who maintain that as soon as the money rattles in the strong box the soul flies out of purgatory."

"They are the enemies of the Pope and of Jesus Christ, who, by reason of the preaching of indulgences, forbid the preaching of the Word of God."

"The indulgence of the Pope cannot take away the smallest daily sin, as far as regards the guilt or the offense."

Luther's act electrified the whole land. News of it seemed to be borne on wings of the wind. In a fortnight, copies of the theses were in every part of Germany, and in a month they had found their way to Rome. They were translated into Dutch and Spanish, and a traveler sold them in Jerusalem. The wildest excitement prevailed. At last the voice had spoken for which men had waited so long. And at the first sound of it the common people, the devout people, monks in their cells and peasants in their cottages, rose up in welcome.

On the contrary Tetzel shook with rage. He prepared theses in reply to Luther's. He stated his hope and belief that the heretic would be burned.

At first the pope smiled upon the papers in amusement. "A drunken German wrote them," he said, "When he has slept off his wine he will be of another mind."

But the pontiff soon found cause to altar his judgment. This new movement was taking shape with incredible speed. In every city and university, Luther's name was becoming known; his action was being discussed and too often approved.

The heretic was commanded to appear before the pope in Rome.

Luther understood that this could well mean his death sentence, for Rome had not the best of names as a center for free discussion, and the justice and mercy of papal judgments were questionable. The summons had come, too, on the heels of a letter he had written to the pope — a letter in which he had kindly explained his position, and had expressed in deep humility his respect and submission to his superior.

"At the very moment I was expecting a blessing," said Luther ruefully, "I saw the thunderbolt fall upon me. I was the lamb that troubled the water the wolf was drinking. Tetzel escaped, and I was to permit myself to be devoured."

Through the kind entreaty of friends, it was finally arranged that Luther should appear, not in Rome, but in Augsburg, a German city.

Thither Luther willingly went, the crowd shouting as he left Wittenburg, "Luther forever! Luther forever!"

"Nay," said the brave man, "Not Luther, but Christ forever!"

Entertaining little more hope of leniency in Augsburg than he would have had in Rome, Luther cried, "I must die! Oh, the disgrace that I heap upon my poor parents! But the Lord's will be done. Even at Augsburg, even in the midst of his enemies, Christ reigns. Let Christ live; let Luther die!"

At Augsburg he met the papal legate, who commanded him in the pope's name to recant.

"I shall apologize," replied the courageous reformer, "as soon as you can show me by the Scriptures wherein I am wrong."

The legate was furious. He threatened, he bribed, he entreated, but nothing would shake the fearless monk. At length, losing his temper, the legate cried, "What! do you think that the pope cares for the opinion of a German boor like you? The pope's little finger is stronger than all Germany. Do you expect your princes to take up arms to defend you? I tell you, no. And where will you be then — where will you be then?"

"Then, as now," replied Luther, "in the hands of Almighty God."

Luther's coolness enraged the legate. "Retract!" he shouted. "Retract! Retract or return no more!"

Luther took him at his word and withdrew. Slipping out of Augsburg at night, he made his way back to Wittenburg, arriving there October 30, just one day less than a year from the day he had nailed his ninety-five theses to the church door.

From this time on, the lightnings already playing on the horizon cracked more and more ominously about the head of the solitary and daring Luther. Enraged at the reformer's obduracy, the pope at once excommunicated him and demanded that he be sent to Rome. However, through the kindness of Frederick the Elector, the trip was delayed. At this, the impatient and furious pope hurled at Luther an imperial edict called a bull, repeating his excommunication, and condemning him and all his works.

When the bull arrived in Wittenburg, the professors refused to post it, but announced instead:

> All friends are invited to assemble about nine o'clock at the church of the Holy Cross outside the city walls, where the godless books of the papal constitutions and scholastic theology will be burned . . . Come, pious and zealous youth, to this pious and religious spectacle, for it is now the time when the antichrist must be exposed.

A large number of students and professors assembled at the east gate of the university campus the morning following. Luther leading the way, they marched outside the town and built a bonfire. When the flames were high and the smoke billowed into the heavens, Luther cast the bull, the edict of the pope himself, into the fire.

"Since thou hast vexed the Holy One of the Lord," he declared solemnly, "may everlasting fire vex and consume thee!"

It was Luther's definite break with the church of Rome.

Influenced and helped by Melancthon, a young scholar of great sweetness of character and of high learning, Luther began to issue his appeals to the nobility, to the clergy and to the people in rapid succession.

"The time for silence is gone," he declared, "and the time for speaking has come."

The pope, too, was busy. He appealed to the new Emperor, Charles V of Spain, urging him to put Luther under the ban of the Empire. On the other hand, the German princes demanded for Luther a fair hearing. Yielding to the latter, he finally called the reformer to appear before him at a Diet he was assembling at Worms, and promised him safe conduct.

Luther's sense of security was not perceptibly strengthened

by the promise. He remembered that safe conduct had been promised John Huss, too, but that had not hindered him from being burned alive!

From the first, however, Luther regarded the summons as a call of God and determined to go.

While the agents of Rome were thus trying their utmost to destroy the reformer, Germany was overwhelming him with acclamations. Although the plague was raging in Wittenburg at this time, new students arrived at the university daily, and from four to six hundred followers and students habitually sat at the feet of Luther and Melancthon. The two churches belonging to the convent and town could not hold the crowds who came to hear Luther preach. Princes, nobles and learned men everywhere wrote him letters of encouragement, consolation and faith.

To a former friend who had grown timid in the heat of the conflict, Luther wrote, "You exhort me to be humble, I exhort you to be firm."

He left Wittenburg on the second of April, 1521. His journey to Worms was a long series of triumphs, in spite of the fact that oftentimes his friends sought to dissuade him, warning him of the grave dangers involved.

"Not go to Worms!" cried Luther, "I shall go to Worms though there were as many devils there as tiles on the roofs."

And to Worms he went — this noble man, alone, strong only in the God whose principles of right he was defending.

At Worms Luther stood before the Diet. Never had man appeared before a more imposing assembly — Charles V himself, and two hundred of his court. For a moment the reformer was somewhat awed. One of the princes, seeing this, whispered kindly, "Fear not them which kill the body, but are not able to kill the soul."

Luther was called upon to recant.

"Unless convinced by the Holy Scripture," said he, "or by clear reasons from other sources, I cannot retract. My conscience is a prisoner to God's Word." Then looking around upon the assembly which held his life in its hands, he added, "Here I stand, I can do no other; may God help me! Amen!"

This was the last word. The council broke up. Many urged Charles to seize Luther and burn him, but to the amazement of everyone he allowed him to go free. From that moment the spell of absolutism was broken and the victory of the Reformation was secured.

A plot was formed to assassinate Luther on his way back to Wittenburg. But the friendly Elector heard of it and sent five horsemen, armed and masked, to "kidnap" the traveler. They rushed upon the wagon in which he was riding, threw the driver to the ground, and dragged Luther from his seat. Throwing a military cloak over his shoulders, the assailants put their prisoner on a horse and galloped away with him into the gloomy glades of the forest, thence to Wartburg Castle. Here the reformer remained for ten months disguised as a knight.

During this time, Luther was not idle. He wrote letters to his friends, heading them as from the "Isle of Patmos," thus comparing his prison to the island to which the Apostle John was banished. He secretly wrote and sent forth many tracts. He translated the New Testament into German. In this work, Luther gave to the German people a "legacy of divine truth which was to be their dearest spiritual guide."

Upon his return to Wittenburg, he translated the Old Testament, completing it in 1532. He also translated hymns and chants, then composed hymns of his own and set them to music. They did much to awaken in the people a new desire for spiritual things. They brought religion down to live with the people in their common tasks, to cheer and console, to become intimate and precious. Christ had come down from the clouds in which He had been hidden and now He tabernacled amongst them.

The Reformation, inaugurated by Luther, marked a crisis in the history of civilization. He inflicted smashing blows against the degradations of the religion of that day, loosing the people from their bondage to the Papist regime, and opening the way for a revival of evangelical and practical religion.

Unavoidably, Luther's attack on the corruption of the Church invited persecution against himself. Every day he carried his life in his hands, "and," says a historian, "one of the wonders of history is that he did not lose it." It was a wild day, full of fury and bloodshed, and in the center of the whirlwind stood the fearless figure of Luther himself. Indeed, the keynote of his life was, "Here I stand!"

He did not fear even the devil, though he fully believed that one had power to do him physical harm. One night he was awakened from sleep by a noise in his room. He rose from his bed, lit a candle, but found nothing. At once he discerned the source of the disturbance. "Oh!" he said, "it is you, is it?" and returning to his bed he soon fell asleep.

Once Luther wrote, "When I go to bed, the devil is always

waiting for me. When he begins to plague me and brings out a catalogue of sins, I say, 'Yes, old fellow, I know all about it. And I know some more you have overlooked. Here are a few extra. Put them down.' " Then he would remind the accuser that all his sins were under the blood, and the struggle would cease.

A favorite story about Luther is that in one encounter with the devil he threw his ink bottle at him. There are inkspots on walls of four different historical "Luther" buildings in as many different towns. The origin of all of them is uncertain. The ink spot in the northeastern corner behind the stove in the "Luther Room" at Wartburg has often been replastered and re-inked. One authority states that in all likelihood the story was invented by the Luther biographer, Ratzeberger, the medical doctor who wrote toward the end of the sixteenth century, plentifully embellishing the Reformer's life with many stories from tradition or his own imagination. Nowhere in Luther's writings, not even the *Table Talks*, is there a reference to throwing an inkwell at the devil, though we can be sure that he would not have hesitated to do so if the idea had occurred to him.

Luther carried in his heart an awful sense of the presence of God, and the fearfulness of sin. To Melancthon he said, "So preach that people will fall out with their sins or fall out with you." He knew the Scriptures and loved them as no other man in his day and generation. He was a man of prayer, spending hours of each day alone with God, carrying his soul apart from the world's busy thrall.

"I will call this Luther a true, great man," wrote Carlyle, ". . . a right spiritual Hero and Prophet; for whom these centuries, and many that are to come yet, will be thankful to heaven."

The scripture revealed to Luther on the staircase of Pilate at the Sancta Sanctorum, brought a light into the soul of Luther that was to be shed over the whole world. To be sure, good works were needed, he granted. But works were not enough. He knew by experience that making holy pilgrimages and kissing the pope would not save a poor sinner. If one were to gain salvation, he discovered, he must do so through living faith in the blood of the crucified Saviour.

"Faith! Faith in the Son of God alone," was Luther's cry. It was through living faith that this repentant, seeking monk found peace to his own troubled soul. And it was this lost doctrine of faith in Christ that he restored to the world.

From Each Sly Moment to the Next

"OH, MISSI," CRIED A dusky-faced chief of the South Sea island, Aniwa, "your head is going wrong!"

The missionary smiled patiently and went on with his work. His attitude only aroused the black man to more insistent argument.

"Missi! Rain comes only from above! Don't let our people hear you talking about going down into the earth for rain. If they hear such a thing they'll never listen to your word! They'll never believe you again!"

"But we need water, Namakei," explained the missionary. "I am going to sink a well down into the earth, to see if our God will send us fresh water up from below."

Namakei turned away with a gesture of futility. He gathered his men together to watch the missionary, lest the white man should try to take his own life or do some other outrageous thing. "Poor Missi," he said to them, shaking his head. "That's the way with all who go mad. There's no driving of wild notions out of their heads. We must watch him now."

John Paton struggled on alone. He knew that if he succeeded in getting water, the well would not only supply a pressing need, but it would also prove to the people that his God, the one true God, is greater than all their gods of wood and stone put together, for their gods had sadly failed to answer their frantic prayers for rain.

Toiling as he was under the tropical sun, the missionary was soon exhausted, unable to dig another shovelful! What should he do? He went to the house and filled his vest pocket with English-made fishhooks. Knowing that these were tempting to the young natives, he bribed them into helping him empty the buckets of dirt as he dug. He gave one fishhook for every three buckets of dirt.

Day after day the work continued, but the hole deepened very slowly.

It was backbreaking and discouraging work. And when, one night, the walls of his twelve-foot excavation caved in, the missionary was in danger of losing not only his well but his helpers, too. No native dared venture into the shaft after this. The white man then devised a windlass by which the workers at his signal could wind up the buckets of dirt and empty them. Finally, a depth of thirty feet was reached, and the missionary whose heart had almost sunk sometimes with the sinking of the well, noticed that the earth and coral seemed to be faintly soaked with dampness.

"Living water! Living water!"

Could it be? Hope that it might be so tugged for dear life at Paton's breast.

"I think that Jehovah God will give us water tomorrow from that hole," he confided to Namakei when the day was ended. But he dared not voice the terror he was tempted to feel that the water might be salt. Thus, tenaciously, he clutched to his heart the faith that in this well God would answer their prayers for water and would manifest His miracle-working power to the heathen.

The chief was not impressed. "No, Missi. You will never see rain coming up from the earth on this island. We wonder what is to be the end of this mad work of yours. We expect daily, if you reach water, to see you drop through into the sea, and the sharks will eat you! That will be the end of it. Death to you, and danger to us all!"

"Come tomorrow," was all the missionary said.

In his heart he knew he was risking much, but he believed God to be leading him on, and more important, he knew he sought God's glory, not his own.

At daybreak the next morning he sank a narrow hole in the center of his well. He went as far as two feet down when he was forced to stop. Water! Water rushed up and filled the hole! Perspiration stood out on the missionary's face. He trembled with excitement! Water! He filled a tiny tin cup and put it to his lips, muddy though its content was. One taste told him the water was fresh! He almost fell on his knees in the mud to praise the Lord.

The chiefs with their men had now gathered at the well. They waited in expectancy. "Missi" next filled a jug which they had seen him take into the well empty. He came to the top with it.

"See the rain which Jehovah God has sent us!" he cried.

They all crowded around in haste, but superstitious fear held them in caution. Only Namakei dared experiment with it. He shook it to see if it would spill. He touched it to see if it felt like water. Finally he tasted it.

"Rain!" he exclaimed in wonder. "Rain! But how did you get rain from down there?"

"Jehovah, my God, gave it out of His own earth in answer to our labors and prayers," the missionary repeated. "Go and see it springing up for yourselves!"

"We are weak with wonder," Namakei whispered. "Wonderful, wonderful is the work of your Jehovah God."

Fully convinced that the well held a real treasure, Namakei and his men eagerly helped "Missi" wall up the well by carrying large coral blocks and squaring them with their own hands.

Strangely enough, though the natives themselves tried after that to dig six or seven wells in their respective villages, they either found coral rock through which they could not dig or found only water that was salt.

"'Missi' not only used pick and spade," they said, "but he prayed and cried to his God. We have learned to dig, but not how to pray, and therefore Jehovah will not give us the rain from below."

The sinking of the new well broke the back of heathenism on Aniwa. It had been a long, disheartening struggle — one that had tested Paton's mettle and faith at every turn.

First, before he had left Scotland, his homeland, for this work, there had been the excruciating leave-taking of his father — the venerable man whose prayers had been a benediction on his life from his infancy. James Paton had walked the first six miles with his son as John set out for Glasgow to commence preparation for his missionary work. When they had parted, the father had given his blessing. Then he had stood on the spot watching till his son was out of sight.

All the obstacles in the way of his getting to the field having been hurdled, John Paton, with his new wife at his side, was plunged into the tragic experiences incident to his missionary career in the South Sea island of Tanna, and later on, in Aniwa. His initiation would have prostrated a weaker man, for it was only a few months after landing that his wife and baby boy succumbed to malaria, and left him a lonely exile in that cannibal island of the far-off Pacific. Despite his breaking heart, he laid the precious dust of his beloved ones in the same quiet resting place, having made their coffins and dug their graves with his own hands.

In hourly danger of attack by the island's hostile cannibals, Paton heroically went on with his work, experiencing many miraculous escapes, often watching his enemies slink away, for no other reason except that, restrained by the hand of the Almighty, they felt powerless to strike him.

He laid his loved ones in the same quiet resting place

The mania of the natives for stealing the missionary's strange belongings, caused Paton much inconvenience and hardship. They ran off with his cooking utensils, his chickens, and even the blankets and sheets he hung out to dry! When he inquired about his lost articles, every last Tannese feigned innocence.

Then one day there arose a great commotion. "Missi, Missi," everyone cried, "there is something coming over the sea and we don't know what it is. Come quickly and tell us what it is. It's smoking like a volcano. Is it a spirit or a god or a ship on fire? What is it?"

Gathering from their excited descriptions that a British battleship was steaming toward Tanna, Paton answered adroitly, "I cannot come out right now. I must dress myself in my best clothes, for most likely what you have seen is one of Queen Victoria's ships coming to ask if your conduct is good or bad, and if you are stealing my property or threatening my life, or how you are treating me."

Stabbed with terror, hearts of the guilty ones beat faster and faster. With one voice they cried out, "Oh, Missi, don't tell the Queen's men. We'll bring everything back to you at once . . . and no one will be allowed to steal again!"

"Then be quick about it," Paton answered seriously, "Everything must be returned before the ship arrives."

Away they scampered in all directions, and soon were back again with pots, crockery, knives, forks, blankets, etc. Paton thanked them for bringing back so many things, and, upon threat of telling the captain of the ship about their misdemeanors, he won their promise that there would be no more stealing from him.

"Our bad conduct is done," they all averred gravely. "We are in black fear."

However, this was not the end of Paton's troubles. Only for short periods was he left unmolested, and he never knew when or where he would be attacked next.

Among the strange superstitions of these people was the belief that their sacred men possessed a power called Nahak, by which they could, if they chose, cause a person to die. But it was supposed to be possible only if they could obtain the remains of food that had been eaten by their victim — a banana skin or an orange peel, for example, over which to chant their incantations. Paton longed to stamp out this superstition. One morning as Paton was pleading with the tribes to forsake their heathen religion and worship the true God, three powerful chiefs, sacred men, defied his pleas.

"We do not believe in your God," they growled, "We have power to kill you by Nahak, if we can get possession of a piece of food you have eaten."

Paton caught at the opportunity to put their statement to the test. He asked a woman standing by for some of the native fruit she carried in her basket. Then calling upon everyone to watch, he took a bite out of three different "plums" and handed the remainder to each of the chiefs.

"You have seen me eat of this fruit," he addressed the whole company. "You have seen me give the remainder to your sacred men. I challenge them to kill me by their sorcery, for I deny that they have any power against me."

The chiefs accepted the challenge, but the rest fled from the place terrified.

"Alas! Missi!" they cried, believing that he would soon be dead.

The chiefs repeated again and again their strange incan-

tations over the uneaten portions of food, glancing wildly at
Paton from time to time to see if he were still alive.

When, after all their efforts, Paton still stood before them
unharmed, they decided to call in all the sacred men of the
island. "Before next Sabbath," they declared, "we will kill
Missi. Let all watch, for he will soon die, and that without fail."

Paton went back to his station. All week long the sacred
men did their utmost to cause his death by witchcraft, daily
sending messengers to inquire about his health. As the days
passed, excitement increased.

The next Sabbath, Paton stepped into the village in more
than his usual health and strength. He found a great crowd
gathered, fear and awe written on their faces, as if they doubted
that it could be Missi himself standing in their midst.

"My love to you all, my friends," he called out. "I have
come again to talk to you about the true God."

The three sacred men admitted they had failed to kill the
missionary by Nahak, giving the artful excuse that Paton himself was a sacred man. When Paton called the people around
him to talk about the true God who hears prayer and protects
His own, one of the chiefs, defiant and angry, marched away.
He soon returned, however, waving his warrior's spear and
pointing it at Paton.

Without any outward show of fear, the missionary continued
to sit calmly, talking of the one true God, and so closely were
the people gathered around the speaker that fear of striking
others kept the chief from throwing his spear that day. For
weeks afterward the thwarted chief intermittently appeared suddenly at Paton's back, his giant spear poised in hand. But it
was never thrown.

The failure of Nahak to kill Paton shook belief in it to some
extent, but it took many, many years to free the people from
their dread of this weird superstition.

Days went on with things growing steadily worse instead of
better. Miaki, the harbor war chief, spent most of his time stirring up hatred against the worship Paton had instituted, and
telling Paton it would not be long before he would be killed.

One day, Miaki and a horde of armed savages were seen
racing down the hill straight for the mission house. There was
not a minute to lose. Paton called a couple of natives who were
with him, and together they fled for their lives. In his haste,
Paton could snatch up only his Bible, his translations and a couple

of light blankets. They plunged into the bush, and finally arrived at a friendly village. A few hours later, a messenger arrived from Miaki saying that it was quite safe for the mission party to return to the mission house. However, knowing how deceitful Miaki was, Paton felt sure this was a trick to lure him back into the clutches of his enemies. To test this, natives went back to the mission house, and on two suceeding nights, Miaki's men surrounded the house in search of Paton. When they could not lay their hands on him, they stole all they could carry away, tore up his books, and made musket bullets out of the type he had used in his printing press.

Seeing that there was no use to stay where his life was constantly in danger and where his presence also endangered the lives of his friends, Paton decided it would be better to turn his face to the Mathieson's station at Aneityum, on the other side of the island. At that time a friendly inland chief was on his way home, which lay in the direction Paton wished to travel, and this native agreed to let the missionary travel with him.

At last they reached Kwamera. Somehow Mr. Mathieson had heard that they were on their way to him, and he and his wife came out to meet them. While waiting for boats to convey them to the Mathieson's station, the three missionaries and their native helpers were surrounded again and again by hostile natives. One evening, worn out by watching, the missionaries fell asleep. About ten o'clock, Paton's little dog awakened him by tugging frantically at his clothes. Men with flaming torches were passing his house. They had already set fire to the nearby church and the reed fence connecting it with the place where the missionaries stayed. It looked as though nothing could save those within, for soon their little house would be in flames, and if they tried to flee they would be massacred by the natives waiting outside. Paton seized a tomahawk, then went out into the darkness, telling Mr. Mathieson to lock the door behind him. While Mr. and Mrs. Mathieson prayed inside, Paton cut down the burning fence and threw it back into the flames.

Savage men crept out of the shadows, certain of their prey. They lifted their clubs to strike. But in that instant, an ominous sound grew out of the southwest. Clubs dropped. The marauders knew what was coming and stood awed, alert. An angry tornado! It was tearing down upon the island at that very moment! On it came with a mighty roar, driving the flames away from the house. Soon torrents of rain descended, putting out the fire entirely. Stricken with fear at this unexpected turn of events, the natives slunk away, mumbling, "This is God's rain! Surely, this is God's rain!"

The next morning a ship came by and took the missionaries on to Aneityum.

Paton's leave-taking of Tanna was a sad one. For four years he had toiled, preached and suffered, seemingly to no avail. Yet surely, all was not lost. Someday he would return and at last see the Tannese become a happy Christian people. In the meantime he planned to spend his days translating the Gospels into Tannese.

However, his fellow missionaries, seeing Paton looking ill and thin, urged him to leave the island for a time, and go to Australia where he could arouse interest in the New Hebrides Mission. After some deliberation and prayer, Paton complied with their request. His trip took him not only to Australia but to Tasmania and even to Scotland. Before his return to the New Hebrides he had raised funds for a mission ship, the *Dayspring*, had enlisted four young men for missionary work in the New Hebrides, and had met and married Margaret Whitecross. When the *Dayspring* sailed back to Aneityum, Paton and his wife were on board. Accepting the decision of the other missionaries, Paton now agreed to go to Aniwa to labor, which was in due time to be the scene of the sinking of the well.

While the building of the missionaries' house was in progress, Chief Namakei often stood by, watching with great interest. One day, Paton, in need of nails and tools, wrote a note on a piece of wood and asked Namakei to take it to Mrs. Paton. "The wood will tell her what I want," Paton explained.

"Oh, Missi," cried Namakei, shaking his head, "you only make a fool of me. Wood cannot talk."

But after repeated assurances that Mrs. Paton would understand, Namakei went off ·and soon returned with the articles needed. Immediately he demanded an explanation. Paton pointed out to him the message and told him that in the same way God could speak to him through His Book when it should be translated into his language and he had learned to read. Eager to read God's Book, Namakei later became Paton's most valuable helper in the work of translation.

Paton's medical work on the island did much to gain the confidence of the natives. Soon, following the example of their chief, they were bringing their girls and boys to the missionaries to be trained as Christians and taught to read. Many of these went out later as evangelists and teachers, taking the Gospel to their own people. Paton soon printed a little Aniwan book containing a collection of scripture passages. A church sprang up, built by volunteer native labor.

After many years of toil on the island, Paton was asked again to travel in the interests of the Mission. He raised funds for a new ship to ply the waters between Australia and the islands, that the missionaries might be better cared for. The result of his speaking and writing was the founding of the John G. Paton Mission Fund. The first missionary to be supported by it was his third son, Frank Paton, who went to Tanna where his father had first worked, and where from each sly moment to the next during his four-year exile there, his life had hung on so slender a thread.

John Paton died in 1907 at the age of eighty-three, but not before he had seen Aniwa become a Christian island, and had witnessed on Tanna the gathering of a Christian congregation. Such was the victorious end of a life so selflessly spent for earth's neglected ones.

Bibliography

Bainton, Rolland H. *Here I Stand.* New York, Nashville, Abingdon-Cokesbury Press. Copyright 1950 by Pierce and Smith.

Benson, Joseph. *The Life of the Rev. John W. De La Flechere.* Chicago, The Christian Witness Co., 1925.

Bingham, Helen E. *An Irish Saint.* Grand Rapids, Michigan, Zondervan Publishing House (reprint).

Bourne, F. W. *Billy Bray, the King's Son.* London, The Epworth Press, 1954 (reprint).

Brain, Belle M. *Love Stories of Great Missionaries.* New York, Fleming H. Revell. Copyright, 1913.

Broomhall, Marshall, M. A. *Hudson Taylor.* London, China Inland Mission, 1929.

Bunyan, John. *Grace Abounding.* Grand Rapids, Michigan, Zondervan Publishing House. Copyright, 1948.

Burns, James and Blackwood, Andrew W., Sr. *Revivals, Their Laws and Leaders.* Grand Rapids, Michigan, Baker Book House. Copyright 1960 (reprint).

Davies, Rev. E. *Frances Ridley Havergal.* Cincinnati, God's Revivalist Office. Copyright 1884.

Davis, George T. B. *When the Fire Fell.* Philadelphia, The Million Testaments Campaigns.

Day, Richard Ellsworth. *So Pilgrim Rang the Bells* and *Man of Like Passions.* Grand Rapids, Michigan, Zondervan Publishing House. Copyrights 1942 & 1955.

Demaray, Donald. *Amazing Grace.* Winona Lake, Indiana, Light and Life Press. Copyright, 1958.

Douglas, Major. *George Fox.* New York, Salvation Army Publishing House.

Edwards, Jonathan. *Life and Diary of David Brainerd.* Chicago, Moody Press. Copyright, 1949 (reprint).

Hodgkin, L. V. *A Book of Quaker Saints.* London, MacMillan and Co., Ltd. Copyright, 1922.

Hubbard, Ethel Daniels. *Ann of Ava.* New York, Missionary Education Movement of the United States and Canada. Copyright 1913.

Jackson, John. *Mary Reed.* New York, Fleming H. Revell.

Morrison, J. A. *Martin Luther.* Anderson, Indiana, Gospel Trumpet Co. Copyright, 1924.

Newton, John. *Out of the Depths* (Autobiography). Chicago, Moody Press (reprint).

Paton, John. *John Paton, Missionary to the New Hebrides,* Volumes I and II. New York, Fleming H. Revell. Copyright, 1889.

Pearce, Winifred M. *John Paton.* Grand Rapids, Zondervan Publishing House. Copyright, 1954.

Railton. *The Authoritative Life of William Booth.* London, Salvation Army Publishing House.

Smith, J. Evan. *Booth the Beloved.* London, Salvation Army Publishing House.

St. John, Ervine. *God's Soldier: General William Booth,* Volumes I and II. New York, The MacMillan Co. Copyright by author, 1935.

Taylor, Dr. and Mrs. Howard. *Hudson Taylor's Spiritual Secret.* Shanghai, China Inland Mission. Copyright, 1950.

Wallace, Archer. *Deeds of Daring.* New York, Harper and Brothers. Copyright, 1934.

Winchester, C. T. *The Life of John Wesley.* New York, The MacMillan Co., 1927.

Winrod, Gerald B. *Martin Luther and the Reformation.* Wichita, Kansas, Defenders Publishers. Copyright by the author, 1935.

Worcester, Mrs. J. H. *The Life of David Livingstone.* Chicago, Moody Press.